Stage
Makeup

Step-by-Step

Stage Makeup

Step-by-Step

The complete guide to: Basic makeup; Planning and designing makeup; Adding and reducing age; Ethnic makeup; Special effects; Makeup for film and television

Rosemarie Swinfield

BETTERWAY BOOKS
Cincinnati, Ohio

A Quarto Book
© 1994 Quarto Inc.

First published in North America in 1994 by Betterway Books,
an imprint of F&W Publications,
1507 Dana Avenue, Cincinnati, OH 45207

Designed and produced by Quarto Inc.,
The Old Brewery
6 Blundell Street,
London N7 9BH

ISBN 1-55870-390-X

Senior editor Maria Morgan
Editor Sandy Ransford
Art editor Clare Baggaley
Designer Clive Hayball
Photographers Paul Forrester, Laura Wickenden
Illustrators Karin Skanberg, Sharon Smith
Picture researcher Susannah Jayes
Picture manager Giulia Hetherington
Art director Moira Clinch
Editorial director Sophie Collins

Typeset by Central Southern Typesetters, Eastbourne
Manufactured in Hong Kong by Regent Publishing Services Ltd
Printed in China by Leefung-Asco Printers Ltd

Contents

Makeup for Theater

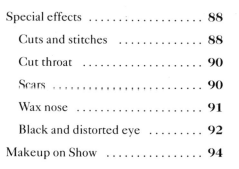

Makeup for Film and Television

Introduction

Welcome to the fascinating, sometimes challenging, but always rewarding world of stage and screen makeup. First you will learn the basic facts about the use of different kinds of makeup. The book is then divided into two main sections: theater – makeup for the stage, from small, intimate cabaret to large shows and ballet; and film and television, where the effects have to withstand closer scrutiny. Within these sections you will find the principles, the application techniques, and step-by-step instructions for the most important makeups for these media, as well as advice on character interpretation and period work. There are guides to applying facial hair, on aging and rejuvenating, on creating special effects such as cuts, burns and bruises, and lots of hints to help you improve your own technique. It is impossible to cover everything, but this book will give you a base on which to develop your own expertise, whether you are working on yourself or on others. Most makeup books are written for professionals; this one is intended for the enthusiastic amateur. Hopefully, it will inspire you to use makeup as it should be used, as part of the whole interpretation of the character.

Whether you are a beginner, or whether you have been in the business for many years, you never stop learning. Advances in equipment and lighting throw up new challenges – if you do not rise to them, your work can easily become dated. You may suddenly see another way of creating an effect, and your expertise will grow a little more. Read right through the book first, to understand the principles as they build through the pictures, then you can dip into sections as you need them. It is a joy to pass on the knowledge I have gained over the years, and I wish you many happy and satisfying hours with your makeup box.

The Role of the Makeup Designer

In the theater and in film and television, the makeup designer has an important role to play, but one that is slightly different in each medium.

In the theater there is an assumption that actors know how to make up their faces; that this was taught at drama school. Increasingly, however, this is a false assumption, so when a character requires special makeup, the actor needs professional help. The makeup artist's role in theater is to design and teach

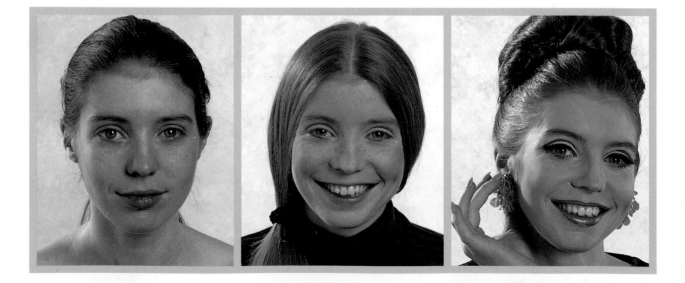

the makeup to the actor. In some countries, professional actors do have the luxury of being made up every night, but this is unusual. It really only occurs when a makeup is too difficult for them to achieve. *The Phantom of the Opera* is an example – all actors playing the title have help with their makeup.

Sometimes a show requires a makeup design for the entire cast. Productions like *The King and I*, where most of the cast need to look Siamese, or *Starlight Express*, where the stylized faces are extensions of the costumes, would be spoiled without a coordinated makeup design. In theatres with resident make-up artists, like the Royal Shakespeare Company in England, the role is to interpret the production designer's ideas and make them work on stage.

Normally in the theater, the makeup artist is involved at the beginning of a production, then the actor takes over. But in film and television, because the face is frequently in close-up, we are needed throughout. In screen work, it is unusual for performers to make themselves up and even if (as with major female stars) they do, the makeup artist will check it. Also, because of the heat of the lights, the face will need constant attention. In films, a wise makeup designer works closely with the chief camera operator, becoming a team to give the best result for the face. On television, the makeup artist is also responsible for hair. We also deal frequently with

people unused to being on camera, so our role involves relaxing them (and sometimes the actors) before they appear. The makeup designer is a major link in a chain which produces the magic of performance.

Preparation for Makeup

It is important to use a toning lotion or astringent (according to your skin type) before applying foundation. It pays real dividends because it removes any stickiness which could disturb the makeup; tightens up the pores, which will help when you remove the makeup; and helps avoid spottiness during a run. Pimples which appear when you are acting are caused by nerves and the amount of adrenaline produced when performing, but can be aggravated by careless cleansing afterward. I am opposed to using moisturizers under theatrical makeup. I think they are unnecessary: on stage you will be producing moisture anyway and any extra will give a shine which will be detrimental to the makeup. Moisturizer also makes water-based foundations greasy. If you must use it, put it on half an hour before.

Removal of Makeup

To keep your skin in good condition, you must remove your makeup properly after every performance. Soap and water are not makeup

Materials

The materials used throughout this book come mainly from the Bob Kelly and Kryolan makeup lines, available from good theatrical suppliers worldwide. The addresses of selected suppliers are given on page 128. The colors often have letter and number codes, but you will soon become familiar with the more commonly used items. These are some of the types of makeup used in the book.

toner and cleanser

TONER AND CLEANSER
Always use a toning lotion or astringent before applying foundation. Unscented baby wipes make fine cleansers for children.

EYES
You will need powder and cream eye shadows in assorted colors.

cream eye shadow

powder eye shadow

LIPS
Have a selection of lipstick colors, including natural shades, matching lip liners, and gloss.

lip liner

lipstick

AQUACOLORS
These come in palettes like watercolor paints; rinse brushes in water.

MASCARA AND EYELINER
Keep assorted colors of block and brush mascaras, together with pencil, cake, and liquid eyeliner.

eyeliner

eyebrow pencil

mascara

cake foundation

SHADER AND HIGHLIGHTER

You need powder, cream and grease shaders in assorted darkish tones. Highlight with cream or grease in lighter shades.

highlight

shader

ROUGE

Use powder for general work, but have some cream rouge (liner) for special uses. Kryolan EF9 liner is used extensively in this book.

powder

POWDER

Use the palest, but not white, professional loose translucent powder.

rouge

fluid foundation

cream foundation

FOUNDATION

This is the basis of the makeups, and is covered in detail on pages 9–13.

solvents and will simply remove the surface material and drive the rest into the pores, eventually causing pimples. You do not need to use a thick, greasy remover; any good cleansing cream or lotion will do the job. If you hate the feel of creams and long for soap and water, use a washing bar, which is cleanser disguised as soap, or cleanse first and wash after.

Foundation

Foundation, like the canvas of a painting, is the background to all your work. I jettison it only if the skin is dark and even in tone, if the actor has a wonderful, smooth and appropriate tan, or if I want the character to look tired or sick. Even in a tiny studio theater, a well-chosen and carefully applied foundation will look fine.

If you are dark-skinned or tanned and need foundation, match the color to your own skin. Otherwise, women should choose a color darker than their own skin for stage makeup, and men need a couple of shades darker than that, or the skin will look soft and feminine. For screen makeup the foundation should be nearer your own coloring unless you are very fair; matching fair skin makes the face look heavy. If you are darker-skinned, never attempt to look paler, or you will end up gray. Redheads and other fair-skinned people may find foundation turns orange on them – if so, use a color a couple of shades lighter than the recommended shade. You will achieve a better result if you use foundation colors designed for the medium rather than an ordinary brand from the drugstore. All theatrical makeup companies suggest colors for certain applications, but they can tend to be very bright and old-fashioned, and it is wiser to go for neutrals. I favor those produced for color television like the Kryolan W line.

Fluid Foundations

These are best for film and television, for both men and women. Kryolan Vistique is the professional brand available; in Europe Clinique is widely used. Fluids in "street" brands may be moisturized or oil-free for greasy skins. Unless you have wonderful skin, they have insufficient cover for stage work.

Equipment

Much of the equipment used here will be readily available at cosmetic counters, but it is a good idea to familiarize yourself with the less common items available from theatrical suppliers. Make sure you have all the equipment you need before starting the makeups.

hair color

hair gel

ready-made beard/mustache

false lashes

natural sponge

TISSUE AND COTTON BALLS

Have a plentiful supply and use 100 percent cotton, especially for special effects.

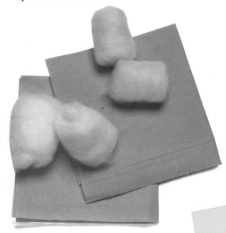

SPONGES

Keep an assortment of natural and synthetic sponges, and a velour puff for powdering. Sponge hair rollers are also useful.

HAIR

You can rent dressed wigs and ready-made mustaches and beards. Crêpe hair or wool comes in long braids. Trim false eyelashes to fit if necessary. Don't forget hairpins and coverings for the hair, and also colored hair sprays, gels, brushes and (long-handled) combs.

BRUSHES

Keep good-quality brushes in a variety of shapes and sizes for different uses.

SPECIAL EFFECTS

These are the main items used: rigid collodion; wax; Leukoflex; spirit gum; latex; "blood."

crêpe hair

latex   *spirit gum remover*   *spirit gum*   *collodion*

Cream Foundations

These are ideal for women, but not for those with greasy skins. They are used for film and television work, but more widely on stage. There are several different types.

1. Sticks: Bob Kelly Creme stick and Kryolan Paint stick – both dense textured for maximum cover and a smooth, velvety finish.

2. Finer textured television stick: Kryolan Face Cream stick – an ideal basic foundation for stage, that can be mixed with fluids to give a lighter finish.

3. Pots: Ben Nye, RCMA, etc. They have a similar texture to television sticks and are good for stage. Some, like Bob Kelly, Mirage and Joe Blasco, were developed for film and television.

4. Compact creams: Vistique, are one step up from a fluid, and are very popular with professional actresses for film, television and stage work.
Note: All creams need powdering well.

Cake Foundations

These are water-based makeups, ideal for men, children and large casts, as they are quick and easy to apply, and are self-setting. They also make the best body makeup. Two types are available.

1. Creamy cake: Bob Kelly Rain Barrel and Kryolan Aquacolor. They may need a little powder. Aquacolor comes in palettes of many bright colors for face and body painting.

2. Dry cake, based on Max Factor Pancake: Bob Kelly and Kryolan Cake Makeup, Leichner Cake Makeup. These are completely self-setting.

How to Use this Book

Main makeups are accompanied by a chart of the face, showing the positioning of the main elements. Each basic element has a key, so familiarize yourself with all the key symbols and read through the introduction and basic principles of makeup on pages 6–11. The following section, on pages 12–29, will take you step-by-step through all the basic techniques, from shading and highlighting to alter the shape of the face, to fitting wigs and moustaches. These are general principles common to stage and screen work. The step-by-step photographic sequences have makeup designs for all occasions. Always read through the routine completely first, and have all the necessary materials and equipment ready before you start. Practice your techniques and adapt them to suit.

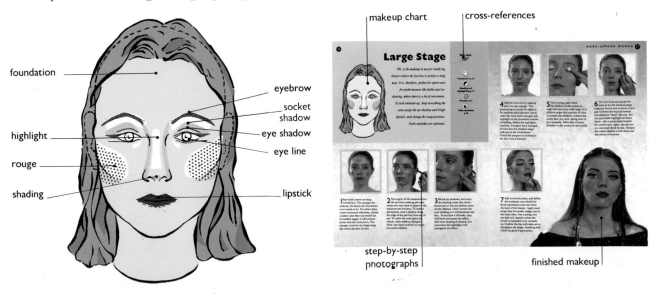

foundation
eyebrow
socket shadow
highlight
eye shadow
rouge
eye line
shading
lipstick

makeup chart
cross-references
step-by-step photographs
finished makeup

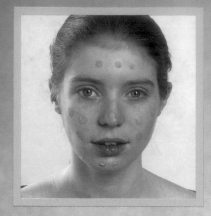

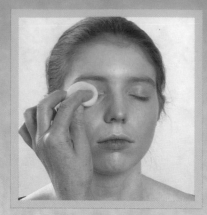

FLUID

1 Pour a little fluid foundation into the palm of your hand, then dot it evenly over the face with a fingertip, remembering to put some on the eyelids and just under the chin. Be careful not to get too close to the hairline. Don't use too much; you can always add more later.

2 Blend the makeup over the entire face with a slightly damp sponge. There are several types available: wedges, round flat sponges, and natural ones. You can, of course, use your fingers, but a sponge gives a better finish. Avoid the lips unless you need to change their shape later. Fade the makeup away under the jaw line to avoid a hard edge there.

3 If you see any redness, apply a little more fluid with the sponge. With very fair skins and/or red-haired people, avoid getting makeup caught in the hairline or eyebrows where it will look orange. When you have finished, the skin should look even in texture.

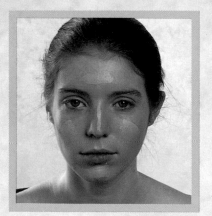

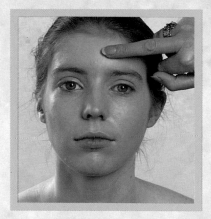

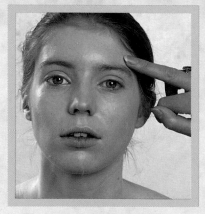

CREAM

1 This type of foundation should be applied initially in strokes to the larger planes of the face – the forehead, nose, cheeks, and chin. With a cream stick, you can just roll it up and apply it directly from the container, but this is unwise if you are sharing makeup. Because creams are strongly pigmented, it is always best to apply them as described to avoid using too much.

2 Blend the cream evenly over the face using a slightly damp sponge or your fingertips. A sponge gives a better result. When you have finished, check to see if you need more. If so, take a corner of the sponge and stroke it onto the cream, picking up just a small amount of makeup. Work this over the areas needing more cover.

3 This is how it should look before powder, with the skin smooth and even. It is easy to use too much cream, so test for heaviness. Finish blending, then run one finger across the forehead. If it leaves a track, you have used too much. To solve the problem, blend further with a clean sponge, then check again. Too much cream can look heavy and flat, and is difficult to keep matte.

CAKE

1 It is important to get the amount of water just right with dry cake makeup; the sponge should drip when squeezed gently. Creamy cake needs a little less water, and you will soon learn how much you need. Always work quickly to prevent the water from evaporating before you have finished, and remember that you can always add more makeup later if you need to.

2 Make sure there is no stickiness on the skin before you start or it will be patchy. Do not apply the foundation too heavily or it will look flat and lifeless. Working quickly, wipe the makeup onto your sponge and place big strokes of color on the forehead, nose, cheeks, and chin.

3 Squeeze out the sponge and blend the cake over the whole face. Dampen the sponge slightly again and add a little more makeup to any places you may have missed, for example, the eyelids and under the eyes. If you are too slow, the makeup will set; once the water has evaporated, it is impossible to even it out. Pat with a tissue and smile hard to ease the tightness.

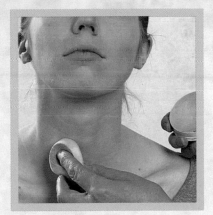

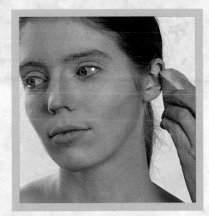

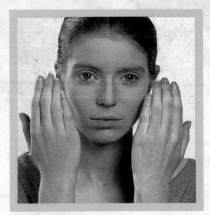

BODY MAKEUP

1 Choose a color to match the face makeup. In some of the professional lines, they have the same numbers. Apply cake with a drier sponge than you used for the face and work in big strokes, blending as you go. When you have finished, pat the area dry with a tissue. If the arms and legs look powdery, polish them softly with a silky scarf.

2 Don't forget to do the ears if they show; they can become red if you are nervous and stand out, especially if they are large, which is distracting for the audience. As they are small areas, you only need a little cake on a fairly dry sponge.

3 It is important to make up the hands, especially for film and TV work. Otherwise, white skin looks very pale and any redness is magnified, while black skin often has much darker pigment on the knuckles, which can be distracting. Work from the fingertips up and bend the fingers to blend the makeup into the lines. Here we see the effect on one hand.

shading and highlighting

To improve or alter facial structure for stage or screen, you must understand the principles of shading and highlighting and how they work under lighting. Shade a feature to make it less noticeable; highlight to draw attention to it. Shade with dark colors, and highlight with very pale colors. It is best to shade first and then highlight. Simple improvements can be done with powder shaders; use creams or grease liners for precision work. Grayish-brown tones are best for shading white skins, and dark browns and black for black skins. Apply shading with a brush a little at a time, but blend with fingertips. Highlighting is done with creams or grease liners. White alone is too strong unless you are using a very pale base or an unusual color, but do not use too much. Without highlights, shading has little effect.

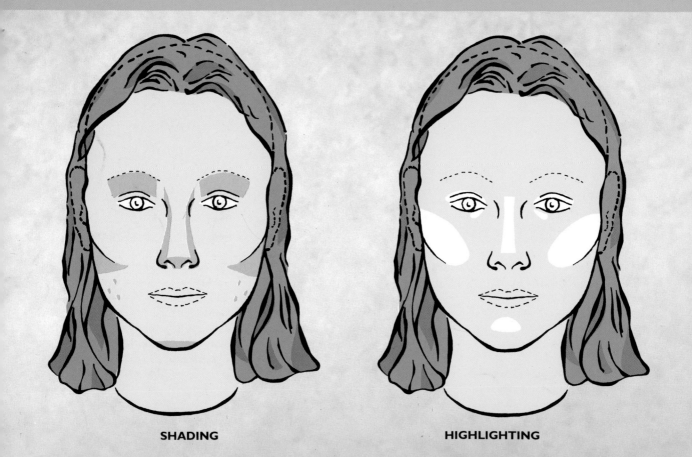

SHADING　　　　　**HIGHLIGHTING**

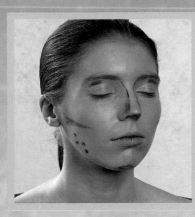

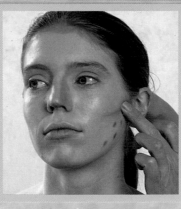

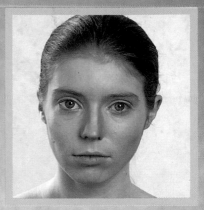

SHADING

1 Shading under eyebrows makes the eyes look bigger, except with naturally large eyelids. Under the cheekbones it adds structure and slims the face. Shading the dotted area improves square jaw lines and broader faces when done with a softer color. Shadows across the point of the chin and over the end of the nose, curving up slightly in the center, shorten long faces.

2 The position of cheekbone shading is vital – in the wrong place, it looks like a dirty mark. Take it from directly in front of the ear (feel for the knotty bit) along the hollow under the bone to where the bone starts upward. Dot a little color at this point and aim toward it. The shadow is curved, with its widest point just in front of the ear. Blend back toward the hairline with a finger.

3 Blend all the shading softly with fingertips. The shading under the eyebrows covers the whole bone area – lift the brows to feel for the right place. Avoid the eyelids. Blending it too close to the nose gives a shifty look. Practice shading the sides of the nose. Don't blend the color too close to the cheeks; it makes the nose shapeless. Cover the nostrils, or you will get a very odd effect.

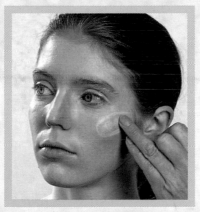

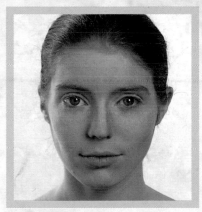

HIGHLIGHTING

1 The basic positions are on the eyelids, in tiredness shadows under the eyes, over the cheek-bones, down the center of the nose, and on the point of the chin. (Feel for the bones under the chin to guide you.) It should only be used for receding or small chins. Put the highlight on with a medium-sized, flat, square-ended brush.

2 Blend the highlight carefully with a sponge tip or fingers, covering the whole lid, smoothing back to the hairline on the cheek-bones, filling in between the shadows on the nose and patting it gently to soften the color on the tiredness shadows. Keep the chin highlight close to the crease. There should be no hard edges when you have finished.

3 The completed shadows and highlights after powdering. The aim is not to change the face dramatically, but to improve its features. The amount used here is suitable for stage work; for film and TV you use less, as the makeup needs to be very subtle.

Thinning the Face

Here we are using basic shading and highlighting to make a face look thinner.

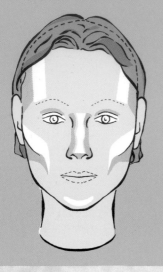

THINNING THE FACE

1 Use a slightly darker FOUNDATION than usual. Apply BASIC SHADING under the cheekbones, but about halfway to the nose, curve down toward the jaw, finishing about level with the mouth. Take temple shadows from the ends of the eyebrows to the hairline in a fairly straight line fading back to the sides of the face. Shade the sides of the nose from eyebrows to nostrils.

2 Blend the shading, working it under the cheek back toward the ear, where it should be at its widest. With a broad face, add more shading on the sides of the jaw line as shown in BASIC SHADING. Blending the shadows with your fingers allows you to feel the bone structure. Unless the makeup is for a really large stage, there must be no hard lines at the edges.

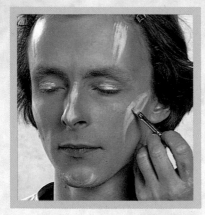

3 Using a square brush, apply highlights to the inside of the temple shadows, the eyelids, down the center of the nose, on the cheekbones following the shadows downward, and on the end of the chin. After blending, the face appears thinner and bonier, and the nose and chin look longer. Accentuate the bump on the nose by widening the highlight there, and powder.

Broadening the Face

Here highlighting is used to make the face appear fuller.

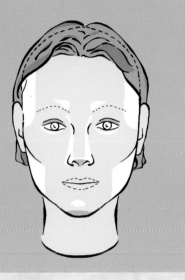

BROADENING THE FACE

1 Use a lighter foundation than usual and dab shading on the eyelids. Take a shadow across the point of the chin, curving up in the center. Women must not use too much shading here or it will look like beard shadow. Repeat this on the end of the nose from nostril to nostril. Using a finger or square-ended brush, blend the eyelid shadow all over the lid, and the chin and nose shadows downward.

2 Add highlights at the temples, then fill in the area under the cheekbones beside the jaw. Add a little highlight on the chin close to the hollow under the lips, but not if the chin is very big. Stroke color on the fullness produced by tightening the muscles under the eyes, and finish with a couple of highlights on the bone just above the inner ends of the eyebrows.

3 Carefully blend the highlights, taking care not to spread them over the shadows. They should be visible but shouldn't stand out as white areas. Powder well. When complete, very thin faces look softer; thin faces seem full; medium faces will appear fat, and naturally plump people will look extremely fat. The hairstyle has also been changed to add width to the face.

Noses

Use shading and highlights to create different shapes of nose, but not for small stage work. Study black and white photographs of real noses, which show the natural highlights and shadows.

THIN, DROOPY NOSE

1 Shade from the eyebrows right down to a point on the tip of the nose, and over the nostrils. Start the highlight between the eyebrows and fill in the area between the shadows.

2 To get a good effect, the highlight must be fairly strong, which makes this a shape best done for large stage performances.

FAT-ENDED NOSE

1 Narrow the top of the nose with shading, then shorten it by shading the end. Feel for the natural fullness on the tip and highlight it, continuing to the tops of the nostrils. Soften the shading and highlights a little.

2 When the makeup is powdered, you can see the effect. The light reflected from the pale areas of the skin will show up the end of the nose and make it look fat.

3 Increase the fatness by changing the shape of the nostrils with a black or very dark brown cake liner. Don't use a pencil – it smudges – and only work on the tops of the nostrils, not all around and definitely not inside them.

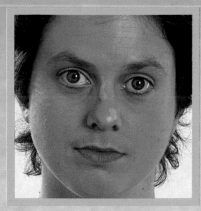
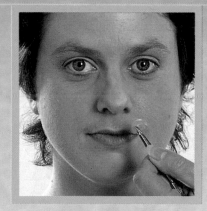
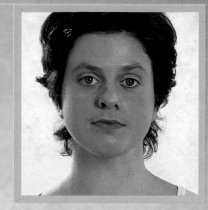

BROKEN NOSE

1 Here the shading appears to push the nose sideways. Apply it further in on one side of the top of the nose, and around one side of the center bone. If the nose has a natural sideways tilt, work toward that. Put the highlights on the edge of the bone shaded, and on the opposite nostril.

2 After powdering, you can increase the effect by inserting a piece of sterile rubber into the nostril you want to look larger. Cut out a little ring of rubber to fit the size of nose. Using tweezers, carefully push the ring only part way into the nose to distend the nostril, or simply darken the top edge of one nostril with cake liner.

3 The finished nose. The highlights emphasize the broken bone and the end of the nose, while the rubber ring inserted into the right nostril distorts it and makes it look larger. To gain the maximum effect, draw the right-hand eyebrow close to the nose, to make it seem further to the right.

Using Highlight

Now we are hiding tiredness shadows and covering scars, spots and other blemishes. Foundation doesn't always hide pimples; cake makeup, which is excellent for greasy skins, will slide over shiny spots, so highlight them away. Always use a brush, as fingers are too imprecise.

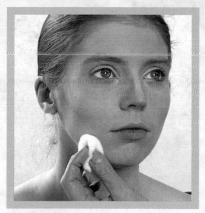

COVERING BLEMISHES

1 With a clean, sterile brush or a cotton swab, put a dab of highlight directly on the spot. Make sure the skin surface is dry or the makeup will not adhere. Pat to blend in using a sponge or cotton swab.

2 Powder with clean absorbent cotton, being careful not to rub off the makeup. It is best to pat on quite a lot of powder and press it into the makeup until the surface no longer looks powdery.

Tiredness Shadows

Tiredness shadows also age the face and, while it is easy to hide them with highlight, take care where you put it.

HIDING TIREDNESS SHADOWS

1 To find the position for highlighting the shadows, drop the chin and look straight ahead. The shadows will show clearly. Paint the highlight onto the gray area only, using a brush. If there are bags to hide, paint the highlight in the dips under them.

2 Lift the head and gently pat the color with your little finger, being very careful not to spread it onto any soft or loose surrounding skin. Pale makeup on the natural highlight under the eye magnifies it and gives bags under the eyes.

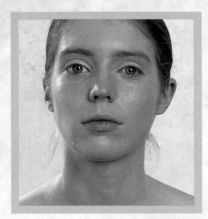

3 Check to see if you have hidden the shadows by lifting the face until the light catches it. If the highlight is correctly positioned, they will have disappeared. This is the best way to check because lighting is often poor in dressing rooms and looking straight in the mirror doesn't always show whether the highlight has worked.

COVERING SCARS

1 To cover an indented scar, take a little highlight on a small brush and paint it into the scar. Avoid getting makeup on the area around the scar, as this would make it look deeper. For a raised scar, do the reverse, brushing the color around, rather than on, it. Always use a brush; fingers are too big.

2 Lightly pat the highlight with your fingertip; then powder carefully. Highlighting inside a scar lifts that area to the level of the surrounding skin; highlighting around a raised scar flattens it to match the skin around it. When the face is lit, the scar should disappear.

Powder

It is difficult to emphasize enough the importance of good powdering – it sets and holds the makeup when you are performing. The most useful powder is loose translucent; with it, you can powder everything from the lightest base to black. It has no color value; it simply sets the makeup. Choose a professional translucent of the palest color, but not white. (Only a white foundation needs a white powder.) Brushes are no good for applying powder for this kind of makeup, as it must be pressed firmly into the base, and this means using a velour puff, a thin, smooth sponge, or cotton balls. If you powder properly, there will be little residue to brush off later. All fluid or cream foundations absorb an amazing amount of powder – don't skimp on it.

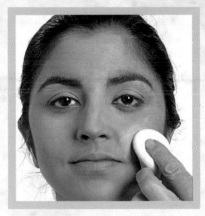

1 Without powder the face will look shiny and unformed, and the lights will find the shiniest areas of the face, show them up, and spoil your efforts. Even with minimum makeup, you must powder if you are using a fluid or cream base. Cake makeup by itself is self-setting, but even that needs a touch of powder in the intermission.

2 If you want a makeup to stay matte and long-lasting, you must press the powder into the foundation. This is difficult to do with a brush, so keep brushes for removing any excess powder after you have finished.

3 The correct way to powder is with a velour puff, a smooth flat sponge, or cotton balls. Do not use cotton balls near contact lenses. A velour puff is best because it holds plenty of powder, and its velvety surface presses the powder firmly into the foundation. Hold the puff or sponge like this and press and roll the powder over the face until all the shine is absorbed.

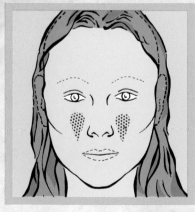

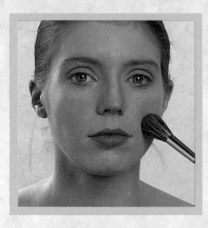

Rouge

Rouge is used for emphasis on the face. Powder rouge or blusher is probably best for general use. For female makeups, stick to peachy tones for an unmade-up look or to show up cheekbones; for period fashion check the color of the time, but be wary of brown tones and bluish shades. Rusty colors work well for men, but use them with discretion. Black skins also benefit from rouge, particularly on stage, as it breaks up the uniform darkness of the skin. Cream rouge, usually called liner, is very useful to create ruddiness, high color, broken veins, tiredness shadows, and as part of the aging process. The one used throughout the book was created for Technicolor film, called EF9, and is made by Bob Kelly and Kryolan. If you can't get hold of it, mix together a clear bright red and a gray-brown. This color is very useful; you can even outline lips with it. For most general work, rouge is applied in these four basic positions.

POSITION ONE

1 This application gives a healthy, unmadeup look. Don't use bright or trendy colors: for white skins, use soft peachy tones for women and children, and slightly darker ones for men. For black skins, use one of the excellent deep rusty colors.

2 This powder (dry) rouge, or blusher, is simple to apply and ideal for the stage, but for film and TV, where sheen is appropriate, a cream rouge would be better. Apply it with your fingers. The position is the same for both types: take the color in long triangles down both sides of the face close to the nose. Powder well before applying dry rouge, or it will streak.

3 If the rouge is in the right place, it will be on the fatness of the cheeks when smiling. It is not a good idea to smile when it is put on, as the rouge will be too far to the sides of the face when relaxed. If the color looks too bright, powder over it, but if you have been really overenthusiastic, use a little foundation to improve matters. If you do this, don't forget to re-powder.

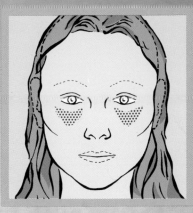

POSITION TWO

1 This is the standard position for normal female makeup in modern productions and where the first priority is that the woman looks good. It looks "madeup" and shouldn't be used for natural faces. It is unsuitable for men, except in elegant costume productions like Restoration plays, and should not be used on children; it makes them look precocious.

2 Powder rouge is best for this. Brush the color over the whole cheekbone area, starting from just in front of the ears. Suck in the cheeks to find the right position, but be careful not to get too close to the mouth. Be wary also of color creeping up over the temples, as it narrows the face. For women, vary the color to tone with the costume; men should use a natural tone.

POSITION THREE

1 This position makes the character look tired. Place the rouge in a v-shape on the center of the cheekbones under the eye sockets, where it emphasizes the pale skin under the eyes, giving the illusion of puffiness. This position is also used for aging.

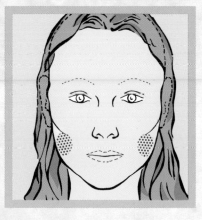

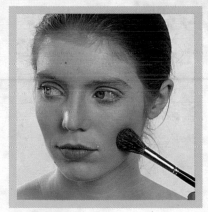

2 When applying rouge in this position, if possible use a small, firm-headed rouge brush, or work with a ball of cotton; you need to be very precise. Choose a natural shade to give a finished effect resembling natural redness. Cream rouge in a brownish-red tone may also be stippled on with a fingertip after the powder to suggest broken veins.

POSITION FOUR

1 Sometimes the face must look heavy or fat. In this case, the rouge should be below the cheekbones, emphasizing the lower part of the face.

2 Apply the color with a big, soft brush in a roundish shape, fading it at the edges with your fingers to avoid a clown-like look. Use a fresh pinkish tone on white skins unless the character is supposed to be tanned. For tanned and darker skins, use a rusty tone.

Using False Hair

These sequences show how to apply and create beards and mustaches. Ready-made pieces come in a variety of styles, colors, and qualities. You can buy hand-knotted ones on fine, hair-lace bases for film and TV work, or cheaper, machine-made types which are fine for the theater. Joke shop beards and mustaches, however, won't do, so keep them for parties. It is fairly simple, and much cheaper, to make you own mustache. This technique is called "laying hair" and for screen work uses real or acrylic hair. However, crêpe hair (wool) is readily available and makes a really good mustache. It can also be used for making false eyebrows by sticking some on a strip of double-sided toupee tape.

See also

Foundation p.12

Powder p.21

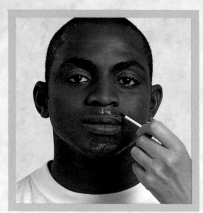

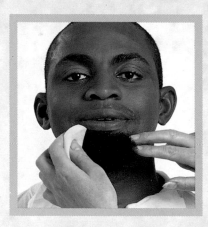

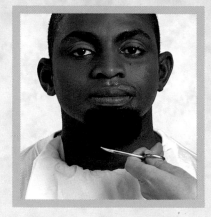

READY-MADE HAIR

1 Put the FOUNDATION and POWDER on the areas where you are going to put the pieces. Paint a layer of spirit gum (not the water-soluble type) in the shape of the mustache above the top lip, and another where the beard is to go, and let them dry. The gum forms a barrier to stop perspiration from disturbing the facial hair.

2 If using both a beard and mustache, put the beard on first. Paint more spirit gum onto the chin and center the beard under the lower lip; then press the sides down, checking that you have enough gum under them. Paint spirit gum under the chin and fit the beard up onto it. To "fade" the lace edge into the skin, use a velour puff or dry sponge to press it firmly along the edges of the beard.

3 If the shape needs altering, you can trim it with nail scissors, but check with your supplier first to see if this is allowed. To improve the shape, spray on a fixing spray or hair gel, and push the hair into the style you want. This isn't usually necessary with good-quality pieces.

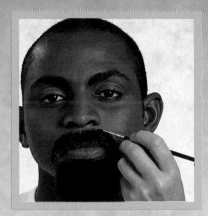

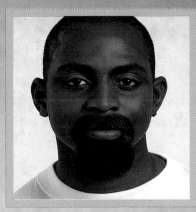

4 Paint more spirit gum above the top lip and apply the mustache. To get it straight, stick the center down first, then work along each side. With most styles it is possible to lift or lower the ends to fit the face. Get the actor to smile as you stick them down; otherwise, you may find it impossible, because the mustache is stuck to the laugh lines.

5 If the shape is uneven or needs altering, use a little cake liner in a matching color to improve it. This is especially helpful if a mustache is crooked and there is no time to take it off and re-apply it. Don't try it for screen close-ups.

6 Here is the finished effect. The eyebrows have been darkened and thickened to match the beard and mustache. As the model is black, the beard texture needs to be slightly curly, like this. Apply whiskers in the same way, remembering to push them well up into the natural hair to avoid a gap.

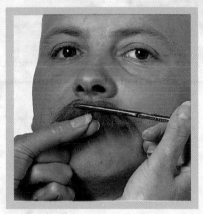

USING CRÊPE HAIR

1 Real mustaches are often a different color from the hair, but for the stage choose crêpe hair matching the actor's hair or wig or the audience will think it is a mistake. Pull out about 3 inches of crêpe hair, and flatten it under a damp cloth or steam iron. Put on the FOUNDATION. Draw the mustache shape you want above the top lip with an eyebrow pencil.

2 Cut the crêpe hair in half, then spread a piece out ready for use. Don't cut the hair too short or it will be difficult to hold. Paint spirit gum along the bottom edge of the shape drawn on the face on one side, then take a piece of hair and angle it with your fingers so that it lies in a natural way and press it onto the spirit gum. Use a brush handle to roll the hair into the gum. Do the same on the other side.

3 Paint another line of spirit gum above the hair and position another line of mustache. The hair usually grows straight down in the center of a mustache, but angles out toward the corners of the lips; follow this pattern with the false hair. Depending on the style, you may need a third layer, which should be shorter than the others.

4 When all the hair is laid, you can trim the length. Snip off a little at a time, or you may cut off too much and spoil the shape. Keep the lips tucked in in case the scissors catch them.

5 Spray a little gel onto the mustache and press it up to give a natural fullness to the hair if required. You can also use acrylic theatrical spray, in which case the mustache can be removed later in one piece and used again. If you use acrylic spray, protect the eyes and nostrils and use short bursts of the aerosol rather than a long spray.

6 You can lay hair onto a layer of latex. Draw the shape, and then paint latex over it, dry it, add a second layer and then apply the hair. To remove the moustache lift up the edge and pull it off carefully, powdering underneath as you go to preserve the latex.

False Eyelashes

Thick lashes, often made of real fur, were fashionable in the 1960s. Adjust lashes by sticking them on the back of one hand and trimming them with sharp scissors. If you have trouble applying full lashes, cut each one into three sections and apply them separately. To ease the fit over naturally curly lashes, curl the false ones around a pencil and wrap them tightly in paper overnight.

1 Make sure the eyelid is not greasy. Put glue on the false lash, raise the chin, and look down the nose. Using tweezers, lay the lash on top of the real ones, pressing down to the roots. Make sure the inner corner is well stuck, and position the outer corner slightly higher than the natural lashes. Press the skin of the lid over the false roots, and apply eyeliner over the strip to cover any glue showing.

2 You can also use half-lashes, going from the center of the lid to the outer corners. Make sure they are natural-looking, not thick or heavy, or they will look strange. Redraw the upper eye line to the inner corners to balance the false roots, and apply a little mascara to blend the real and false lashes.

Hair-lace Wigs

A hair-lace wig is usually the best you can get, but the net front can be daunting to the uninitiated, and seeing a frilly edge distracts the audience. You need to know how to apply this type of wig properly.

1 Our model has very little hair but, before you start, cover thick hair with a wig net or stocking-top. Make sure you have completed the makeup first, because if you get foundation or powder on the hair-lace, it will show.

2 Always put the wig on from the front of the head, with the lace over the eyebrows, then move it up the forehead to the correct position. Check the back and make sure the wig is on straight.

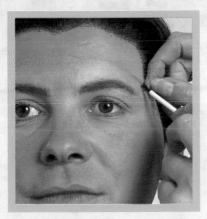

3 When it is in place, there will be two flaps of net in front of the ears to be glued down. Lift the flaps, and paint spirit gum on the skin underneath. Then, holding a flap in each hand, stretch them down as far as possible and press them onto the glue to tighten the lace across the forehead. Hold them in position until the glue dries, then lift the edges of the lace and paint dots of gum underneath it.

4 Press a dry sponge or velour puff along the hair-lace edge. When glued down, the net will seem to disappear into the skin. If the edges of the flaps are exposed, make sure that they are well glued to the skin. Big wigs may need a bobby pin behind each ear for extra hold.

5 With short wigs like this, you can brush the hair into shape and spray it. Bigger wigs, like female ones, are usually prestyled and full of pins, which means that you can only comb the edges a little or you will destroy the set. Remove the spirit gum with a special remover.

Lighting and Gels

In screen work the lighting is usually adjusted for close-ups, so, as long as you understand the basic makeup principles and use the correct colors, you can leave the rest to the chief cameraman. On stage, however, everything is affected by the lighting. In a typical theater, the top lighting and the footlights make you look paler, unless you are tanned or naturally dark-skinned. Top lighting hollows the whole eye socket, and you should avoid shading on the browbone. Footlights take the shape out of the face, and the colored gels used on the lamps can do odd things to stage makeup. Neutral colors remain the same under all lighting.

PEACH
This is the face lit by a gel called Peach Special. It is a very flattering color which warms the skin tone without altering anything in the makeup.

BLUE
A blue gel changes the red tones, making the blusher seem pinker and the lipstick darker. Blue or green eye shadow would appear lighter. The skin tone becomes cold-looking.

RED
Red gels absorb all the blusher and shading and make the lipstick look pale. Green eye shadow appears much darker, blue becomes dark gray and lilac turns black.

GREEN
A green gel darkens the lipstick – if the model wore a deeper red, it would become very dark. The blusher loses strength, but the shading is not absorbed. Green eye shadow pales, blue turns dark green, and lilac becomes almost black.

Eye Shapes

Very few of us have perfectly shaped eyes and these are just some of the variations. Use these examples to adjust your natural eye shape or to create new shapes for specific makeups.

IDEAL EYES

This is the ideal eye shape, perfectly proportioned. However, most of us have eyes that are too round or too narrow or that droop a little, so we have to adapt the basic eye makeup to suit our own eyes. Here is how to do this: the diagrams show the most common shapes and how the makeup changes. I have used the colors from the section for white skins, but choose what is suitable for you.

ROUND EYES

Shade the browbone and blend the eye shadow over the whole eyelid. Take the socket shadow from halfway across the edge of the browbone to just over the end of the eyelid to balance the roundness. Don't take it right across or it will make the eyes look very round. Draw the underline in the same position as for the ideal eye, but leave a gap in the center, to improve the shape of the lower eyelid.

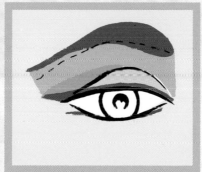

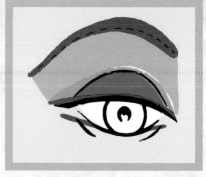

NARROW EYES

Here it is important to shade the whole area where you can feel the bone under the eyebrow; if this is pale, it will make the eye look small on stage. The eye shadow should cover the whole eyelid. Feel for the eyeball under the skin as you blend. You will see the color above the crease if you have done it right. Put the socket shadow along the edge of the eye shadow, and draw the lower line slightly below the edge of the bottom lid.

DROOPY EYELIDS

For droopy lids or those with a strong bone crossing the outer corner, shade the browbone to prevent it from dominating the eye. The eye shadow covers the whole eyelid but, as for the round eye, the socket shadow starts from halfway across the eye. A strong bone at the outer corner makes it difficult to extend the top eye line, but if you round the top edge of the extension, it will fit better. The bottom line is the same as for the ideal eye.

LARGE, HEAVY-LIDDED EYES

This type of eye needs rebalancing because the lid is too prominent. Use highlight, rather than shading, on the browbone to make it more noticeable. The eye shadow should be dark gray or brown to make the eyelid less noticeable. This is the only eye shape that can afford to use a thicker top eye line, which also helps to make the lid look smaller. The lowest line is the same as for the round eye shape.

Makeup for Theater

The first real stage makeup was developed in the mid-nineteenth century by a German opera singer called Ludwig Leichner. Some people think makeup today is heavy and thick like the old greasepaint, and that using it is old-fashioned, but they are wrong. Today there is a vast choice of products available, and not using it is selling the audience – and yourself – short. Lighting changes the way the audience sees your face, often emphasizing the wrong points, but good stage makeup uses the light to give the finishing touch to all the work you have put into building up the character.

Makeup for Women — Small Stage

This is a straight makeup suitable for small and intimate theaters, and cabaret, where the audience is really close. It gives an attractive but made-up look. If you want to look unmade-up, change the rouge position, use highlight as eye shadow, and choose a natural color for the lips. This makeup is also suitable for parties.

See also 👉

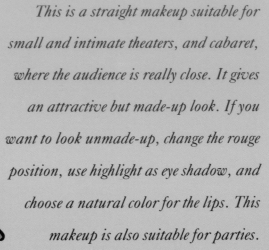

Cream foundation p.12

Shading and highlighting p.15

Powder p.21

Rouge p.22

Lighting p.28

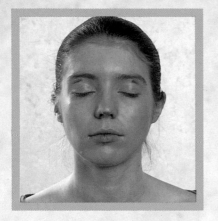

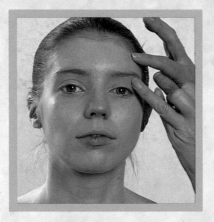

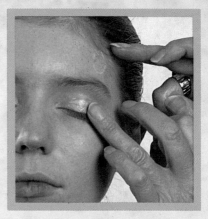

1 Apply a light amount of fluid or fine-textured cream FOUNDATION with a sponge to an even finish. With a little shader on a brush, put a stroke of color under the eyebrows on the browbone, and another across the end of the nose running from nostril to nostril. These are the only shadows from the basic SHADING and HIGHLIGHTING used close to an audience.

2 The shading on the browbone reduces the natural paleness there, which takes the emphasis away from the eye. Blend it softly over the whole bone area. When the makeup is finished, this balancing shadow will seem to disappear, but it makes a big difference to the apparent size of the eyes. Blend the nose shading, curving up slightly over the tip to improve the shape.

3 The larger the eyelids, the larger the eyes will appear. Dark, smudgy eye shadow makes all but the largest eyes look smaller; instead use pale neutral colors like this gray-green. On black and darker skin tones, bronzes and lilacs look good. Take the shadow over the entire eyelid, everywhere you can feel the eyeball under the skin. Powder shadow should be applied later, after powdering.

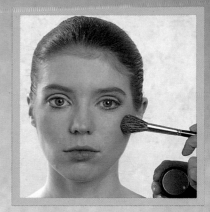

4 POWDER the face carefully. Don't forget the eyelids; cream eye shadow will streak without it and powder shadow will be difficult to blend evenly. Take a fine line of powder shadow along the roots of the lower eyelashes right across under the eyes, using dark brown, except with black hair. Don't go right up to the corners. Straighten out when you reach that point, but don't extend the line.

5 A socket shadow gives further definition. Use the same color as you did under the eyes, but apply it with a bigger brush. Lift the eyebrows and feel for the edge of the eye socket, brushing the shadow along it in a soft, roundish curve to give a soft mist of color, not a hard line. If you can't see it when you look in the mirror, it is too low and has disappeared into the crease of the lid.

6 Brush ROUGE over the cheek-bones and in the hollows underneath to emphasize the cheekbones and add warmth to the face. White skins need a peachy tone; olive skins a deeper, more rusty shade; black skins a rich, dark color. Beware of anything blue toned, as it can change under the LIGHTS and GELS. If the rouge streaks, the foundation hasn't been powdered properly.

7 Finally, apply lipstick with a brush, filling in the whole shape and working from the outer corners toward the center of the mouth. You can outline the lips with lip liner, but be sure it doesn't show when you have finished. The color depends on whether you want the mouth to look made-up or not, but avoid brown- or blue-toned lipsticks which don't work well under lights.

Medium Stage

This is the most important stage makeup for all women over sixteen. It doesn't change the way you look – it simply improves the face and gives the appearance on stage of wearing a little makeup. To change this to an unmade-up look, use highlight for eye shadow, change the rouge position to natural, and use a soft, peach-toned lipstick.

See also

Foundation p.11

Shading and highlighting p.15

Powder p.21

Rouge p.22

1 Choose a FOUNDATION to give an even skin tone. When you have applied it, there should be no pink areas on the face. Then apply BASIC SHADING. Here the model has shadows on the browbones, sides and tip of the nose, and under the cheekbones.

2 Blend the shading carefully with your fingers or the tip of a sponge, feeling the bone structure as you go to guide you. The areas you shade will be less noticeable under the professional lighting.

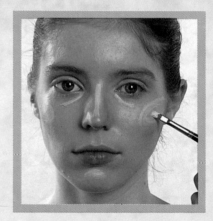

3 Add the HIGHLIGHTS. Remember that the areas you highlight will appear more noticeable on stage, with the exception of the tiredness shadows, which will disappear. When you have blended the highlights, you should be aware of them, but there shouldn't be a striped effect. They will diminish slightly after POWDERING, and you should allow for that.

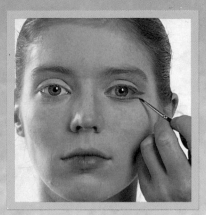

4 Use pale gray-green cream eye shadow and POWDER well. Draw a fine line of cake eyeliner along the top eyelid in the roots of the lashes, extending in a narrow triangle straight out at the corner. Fade the lines down to the inner corners. Take a straight line all along under the eye, beyond the outer corner but not as far as the top line. If you make a mistake, highlight over and re-powder.

5 Mascara and socket shadows make a huge difference to the apparent size of the eyes. Do one eye at a time to see how you are going; the finished eye should look much bigger than the other one. If it doesn't, check back to see what you've done wrong. The most common mistakes are too thick a top line, especially in the center, and curly extensions to the lines.

6 Add ROUGE to emphasize the cheekbones; curiously, the highlight you applied earlier will work through it. Take the rouge over the shading under the cheekbones, too. If you feel at this point you should have used more shade, brush a little brownish blusher into the hollows.

7 For this size stage, you need a stronger lip color for it to be noticed, which means a clear red. Beware of plummy colors or brownish-reds; they don't work well under theatrical lighting. You may do a rather round, old-fashioned shape at first, but if you work from the outer corners in, this won't happen. The bigger the mouth looks, the better, unless it is naturally very large.

Large Stage

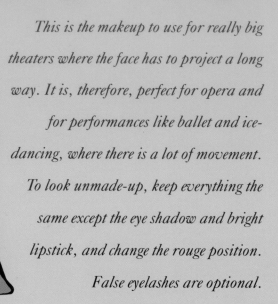

This is the makeup to use for really big theaters where the face has to project a long way. It is, therefore, perfect for opera and for performances like ballet and ice-dancing, where there is a lot of movement. To look unmade-up, keep everything the same except the eye shadow and bright lipstick, and change the rouge position. False eyelashes are optional.

See also

○ **Foundation p.12**

◑ **Shading and highlighting p.15**

▦ **Powder p.21**

False eyelashes p.26

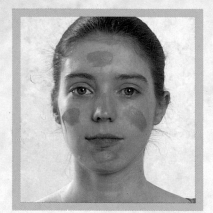

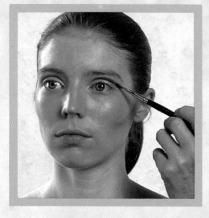

1 Start with a more covering FOUNDATION. The stronger the makeup, the better the foundation cover needs to be. For white skins, unless instructed otherwise, choose a darker color than you would use for smaller stages; it will contrast better with the HIGHLIGHTS. The stronger LIGHTING on a large stage also drains the face of color.

2 Now apply all the shadows from the previous makeup plus any extras you may need to improve the structure [SEE SHADING]. To reduce plumpness, draw a shadow along the edge of the jaw line from ear to ear. To make the eyes stand out clearly, their makeup changes a little; use cream eyeliner to create the socket shadow.

3 Blend the shadows, but leave the shading under the cheek-bones and on the eye sockets quite clearly defined. Don't overdo the nose shading or it will dominate the face. To see how it all looks, step well back and assess the effect. Add more shading if needed, but remember the highlights will strengthen its effect.

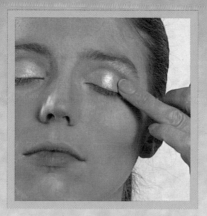

4 Add the HIGHLIGHTS, making sure you use enough. The positioning is exactly the same as for medium-sized theaters, but to make the eyes much stronger, use highlight on the browbone instead of shading. Soften the highlights carefully, but leave more strength of color than for medium-stage makeup on the cheekbones. Check the progress by looking at the face from a distance.

5 Use a strong, pale cream eye shadow on the eyelids to make the eyes look really large. It is difficult to get this intensity of color in powder eye shadows. POWDER the whole face very well, taking time to do it properly. Add a dab of pearly shimmer to the center of each eyelid.

6 The eye lines are exactly the same as for the medium-stage makeup, but be sure to leave a clear gap between the top and bottom extensions to "open" the eye. You can put a little highlight between them – this is particularly helpful for narrow eyes. Again, do one eye at a time and check its size. Deepen the socket shadow a little more and add plenty of mascara.

7 Add FALSE EYELASHES, and define the eyebrows very clearly for facial expression to be seen from the back of the theater. Apply more rouge than for smaller stages, but in the same color. Use a strong, but not dark red, lipstick unless the mouth is supposed to be unmade-up. Outline the lips with dark red to strengthen the shape, finishing with a little lip gloss if appropriate.

African-American Women

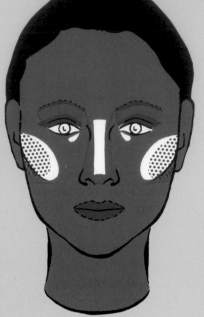

The makeup routine for black skins is almost the same as for white – only the colors change. All the advice given in the Basic Principles on pages 11–23 applies here as well. However, there are a couple of differences: the natural shine of the skin, and its uniform darkness.

See also

 Foundation p.12

Shading and highlighting p.15

Powder p.21

Rouge p.22

1 The FOUNDATION should match the skin exactly. If the face is unevenly pigmented, use a foundation from one of the black street makeup lines designed especially. SHADE the face with either a brownish-black or black, depending on the darkness of the skin, and HIGHLIGHT with a yellowish tone which suits black skins. The positions are the same as for basic female makeup.

2 As the natural shine will be picked up by the lighting and will take the structure out of the face, it is important to POWDER well. Don't use a dark powder; it will cover the highlights and make the face look flat. Instead, try a pale, translucent, loose powder to set the makeup; the paleness will disappear.

3 The best eye-shadow colors on stage for black skins are warm copper tones, or, as here, lilacs. They enhance the eyes without shouting color. For an unmade-up look, use a little powder shine. Choose the eye-shadow color from a black fashion brand – they have more intensive pigments and show up more clearly. Take the shadow over the whole eyelid.

4 Here one eye has been made up with black eyeliner, dark charcoal socket shadow, and black mascara, making it look much stronger than the other one. The eyebrow appears to frame the eye, whereas the other one looks too thin. The eyes are naturally large, but the makeup really increases their size. For more details on creating large eyes, SEE PAGE 29.

5 Dry ROUGE or blusher will lift the uniform darkness of the skin. Strong rusty shades, such as Dark Technicolor, are available in the professional lines, and the black fashion brands have others. Apply it in the appropriate position for the stage size.

6 Don't use bright shiny colors on the lips unless you are creating a glamorous look. A deep red from a fashion brand is best; it shows up the lips without making them too prominent.

7 Here we see the completed eye makeup. Aim to make the eyes dominate the face, to draw attention away from the lips.

Oriental Women

This make-up is very similar to that for white skins – the main differences being the eye makeup and skin tone. While this sequence illustrates the medium-sized stage version, it is easily adapted to smaller and larger stages.

See also

Foundation p.12

Shading and highlighting p.15

Powder p.21

Eye shapes p.29

False eyelashes p.26

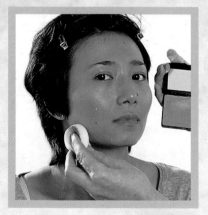

1 If the skin color is naturally deep, match the FOUNDATION to it. The professional lines don't always have the color you need, so try one from an everyday makeup brand, remembering that it must give good cover. If the body tone is the same as that of the face, you won't need makeup on the hands and neck.

2 Oriental women tend to have broad cheekbones and flattish noses, so SHADING is important. Use a clear, dark brown unless the skin is really dark, in which case you will need a brownish-black. Shading the browbones is vital to make the flatness disappear and the eyelid look bigger.

3 For the HIGHLIGHTS use a pale, yellow-toned cream stick makeup such as Ivory or G-G, which work well on olive skins. If you can't find a good shade, mix a little yellow liner into any really pale foundation and use that. Put highlights on the cheekbones, into the tiredness shadows, and down the center of the nose to "lift" the bridge. POWDER the whole face carefully with translucent powder.

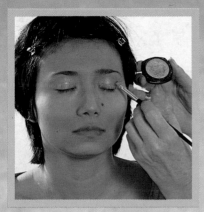

4 Soft-toned eye shadows are the most flattering. This is pewter, but a soft lilac would also be good. Set the lids with powder before applying powder eye shadow, and apply it everywhere you can feel the eyeball under the skin to give maximum size.

5 Now line the eyes, using the EYE SHAPE section for guidance. Don't go right around the inner corners or join up the lines at the ends or the eyes will look very narrow. Keep a good gap between the line extensions to open up the eyes – for large stage work, you can put a little highlight between the extensions.

6 Take a socket shadow along the top edge of the eye shadow, using a powder brown to give the eyelid edge definition without hardness. Run your finger above the lid on the edge of the bone to find the correct position. Mascara the eyelashes and, for a large theater, add FALSE LASHES – the feathery kind are best.

7 Shape the eyebrows elegantly. If they are left short, the browbone will look too strong and detract from the eye. Add a warm, rusty-toned blusher to the cheek-bones. Finish with a clear, soft-colored lipstick. Red is too bright because the lips are usually quite full. Avoid lip gloss for the same reason.

Hispanic and Indian Women

These are makeups designed to enhance the natural facial features for a medium-sized stage and are easily adaptable for smaller or larger stages, using the same techniques as for white skins.

See also

Foundation p.12

Shading and highlighting p.15

Powder p.21

Rouge p.22

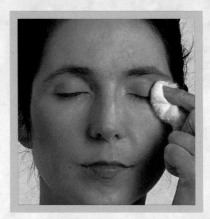

1 If the skin is fair, use a Caucasian FOUNDATION shade, but for olive skins match it to the skin tone. SHADE and HIGHLIGHT the face, and POWDER, omitting the eyelids if you are using cream eye shadow. Brush a deep, peach-toned powder blusher over the cheekbones, taking a little into the shading below to soften the brownness. For an unmade-up look, refer to the ROUGE section.

2 With dark brown eyes a soft lilac eye shadow looks very good on stage. This is a cream shadow which needs powder on top of it. If you prefer powder shadow, you must set the foundation on the eyelids before you apply it, or it is difficult to get an even finish.

3 Draw the eye lines with a black pencil or liner, the top one first, extending as a narrow triangle from the outer corner, then the bottom one, with a shorter extension. The model has strong bones close to the outer corners of her eyes, which make it difficult to get perfect eye lines. To fit the extension to the eye, round the top edge slightly.

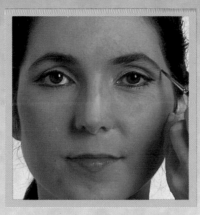

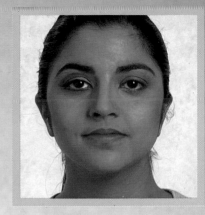

4 One eye is finished, complete with dark brown socket shadow and black mascara, and looks twice the size of the other. Making up one eye at a time helps you to see if you are getting the shape right. If the made-up eye doesn't look bigger, you are doing something wrong. The most common mistake is getting the extensions too close together, or worse still, joining them up.

5 Adjust the eyebrow shape with a pencil or cake eyeliner; if they are naturally dark and a good shape, just brush them through, to lift the hairs, and add a little shine with petroleum jelly. Finally, add a clear red lipstick to look made-up. The edge of the mouth has been colored with a dark brownish-red lining color.

▮ Choose a cream FOUNDATION with good cover, matching the face. SHADE and HIGHLIGHT using a dark brown cream liner and an ivory highlight, and POWDER. Use pewter eye shadow as here, or lilacs or bronzes. Add black eye lines and a charcoal powder socket shadow. Shape the eyebrows and finish with a rusty-toned blusher and a clear red lipstick. Hide patches of dark skin with a camouflage cream.

Makeup for Men — Small Stage

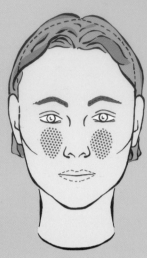

This makeup is for small, intimate theaters and cabarets, where you need as little as possible. You need some, because lighting drains the skin color, even in a small venue, but all you need is foundation. The make-up on our black model adds definition to the face on a medium stage.

See also

○ **Foundation p.13**

◑ **Shading and highlighting p.15**

◉ **Powder p.21**

1 This is how our model looks naturally and, even after makeup, the aim is for a natural look. Do not use too much; you can always add more makeup later if you need to.

2 Pat skin tonic over the whole face with absorbent cotton to remove any stickiness from the skin; it makes cake makeup tricky to apply evenly. The tonic helps to tighten the pores and keep the makeup matte.

3 Stroke FOUNDATION on all the large areas of the face before you begin to blend. If you work on one section at a time, you will end up with an uneven, patchy look. If you go seriously wrong, you may have to clean it off and start again. Don't forget the ears, neck, and hands. For eye makeup for men, see the next section.

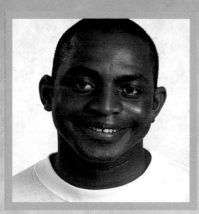

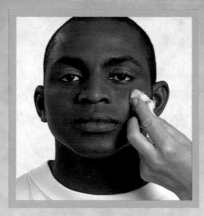

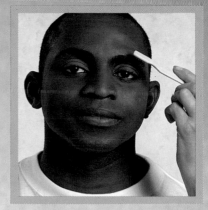

1 If the skin is in good condition with even color, you won't need a FOUNDATION. Otherwise, choose a color to match the skin, using either a cream base or a thin cake makeup. Apply it over the whole face and blend it under the chin. Apply a cream HIGHLIGHT to the eyelids, choosing the same color tone as in the female section. Dab highlight on each lid and blend over the whole eyelid.

2 POWDER the whole face with loose translucent powder, remembering to set the eyelids. The powder will reduce the shine on the skin but leave a slight sheen. If you used cake foundation, you will only need to set the eyelids.

3 Brush through the eyebrows, adding a little black pencil or cake mascara to strengthen the shape if they need more color. Draw a fine line of black along the edge of the lower eyelid in the roots of the eyelashes to define the lower lid [SEE FOLLOWING PAGES].

Medium Stage

See also
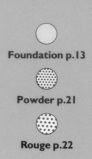

This makeup is suitable for most traditional theaters and concert halls, where the audience is farther away and more detail on the face is needed. When you are familiar with the routine, it should take no longer than 10 minutes to apply.

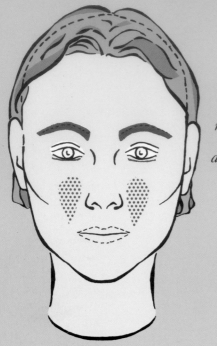

Foundation p.13

Powder p.21

Rouge p.22

1 Choose a FOUNDATION shade and apply it as described in the previous makeup. If you can't see the eyelids in the mirror, or they look narrow, the eyes will look small on stage and the audience won't see them clearly. Dab highlight on each lid to make the eyes look larger.

2 Blend the highlight over the whole lid area, everywhere you can feel the eyeball. Lifting the chin will help you get at the eyelid more easily. When you have finished, the lid should look pale, not white, and it will appear larger. If you have narrow eyelids, it is all right to let the highlight show above the crease of the lid.

3 POWDER the eyelid well with the chin still up. Wearers of contact lenses should use a thin sponge to apply the powder, as cotton fibers can get under the lenses and cause considerable discomfort. Remember you must powder any creamy areas on the face.

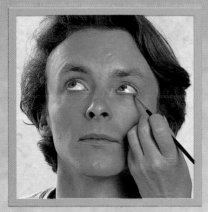

4 Define the lower eyelids with a fine line drawn along the roots of the lower lashes with a well-sharpened pencil or cake eyeliner and a small damp brush. Use dark brown for fair to dark brown hair or wig, black for black hair. Look up and draw the line with little joining strokes under the eyelashes, making sure that you don't go right up to either corner. Fade the line with your finger if it looks heavy.

5 If the eyelashes are fair or look powdery, they will need a touch of mascara. For men use the old-fashioned block type. The roll-on types contain fibers to thicken and extend the eyelashes as well as darkening them, and this makes male lashes look too pretty. Wet the brush to use this kind of mascara.

6 To darken the eyebrows, rub the mascara brush gently on a tissue and, with the color that is left on it, brush through the brows, working from the ends inward. This way you will just touch the hairs and the effect will be very natural. If you need more than that, you will have to use a pencil or cake liner [SEE PAGE 49].

7 Finally, add a soft amount of dry ROUGE in position 1 to give the face more color. A tanned or rosy-colored skin may not need rouge, but pale men will look better for it. Apply the color with a big fat brush. Use just a little and see if you need more; it is easier to add more than to remove it.

Large Stage

This make-up is designed to be used in large theaters for opera, ballet, and ice-dancing, or in any situation where there is quite a distance between the performer and the audience. It works well in performances with continual movement where the eyes need extra definition. Apply a little more of a slightly darker base for this makeup than you would for small and medium-sized theaters.

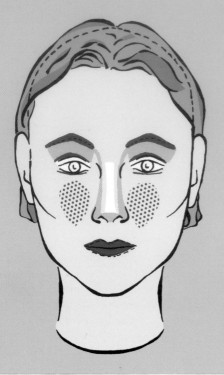

See also

Foundation p.13

Shading and highlighting pp.15, 20

Powder p.21

Rouge p.21

1 After applying the FOUNDATION, add these shadows to the browbones and end of the nose. For others, see SHADING and HIGHLIGHTING. Dab the shading between the eyebrows and eyelids, lifting the eyebrows to help to get it in the right place. Take the nose shadow across the area between the nostrils. Don't use the browbone shading for heavy eyebrows.

2 Blend the shading on the browbone, taking care not to work it into the eyebrow hairs or the model will look like Groucho Marx! Don't take the color onto the eyelids either, or the eyes will look smaller. Wipe your finger on a tissue to remove any excess shading as you blend. Soften the shading on the nose, taking it in a curve over the tip and down between the nostrils. Don't overdo it.

3 Add highlights to the eyelids and down the center of the nose. If the face needs more structuring than this, see SHADING and HIGH-LIGHTING. Only use highlight under the eyes to hide tiredness shadows or to give a younger look.

4 We have added more shading down the sides of the nose. Blend the highlights over the whole eyelid area and down the nose following the bridge, fanning out the color a little at the end. Be careful it doesn't become too wide and avoid taking it up between the eyebrows. POWDER the creamy areas to a matte finish; otherwise, the face will become greasy.

5 Draw eye lines under the lower lashes as in the previous make-up. Then, looking directly ahead, feather a soft shadow of diluted cake liner or powder brown along the socket bone directly above the eyelids with a soft brush to define the edge of the eyelid. It is particularly good for bald-looking eyes. A fine line along the edge of the top lid helps to define pale eyelashes [SEE PAGE 35].

6 Mascara the top and bottom eyelashes. If the eyebrows are thick, they won't need shaping, but you could place a small highlight under the center of the brow to lift the heaviness away from the eye. If, as here, they need more definition, draw little hair-like strokes with a pencil or cake liner among the natural hairs, using a matching color. Take care, as it is easy to overdraw and spoil the makeup.

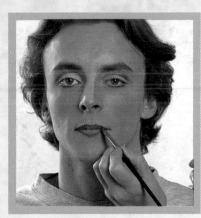

7 Apply the ROUGE in the same position as before, perhaps using a little more. Men shouldn't use lipstick, but the lips need defining. Pale lips are improved by rubbing a little brownish-red lining color over them with a fingertip; warmer-toned mouths just need the outline drawn in with brownish-red or dark red lip liner. Finally, fade the edge with a finger.

Makeup for Children

On stage, children should look like children and not like miniature adults. Little girls, in particular, are often over made-up with too much eye shadow and bright lipstick. Use cake makeup for young faces; it is quick to apply and easy to remove. Talk children, especially boys, through the makeup to help keep them still.

See also

Foundation p.12

Highlighting p.15

Powder p.21

Rouge p.22

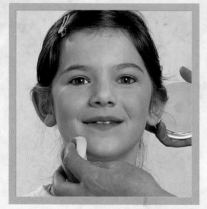

1 Apply a fine layer of cake FOUNDATION with a sponge. Girls with dark or BLACK SKINS will need a cake makeup to match their natural color; preteen caucasian skins are often quite fair, so choose a pale female shade – the sort of color suitable for 19th century women [SEE PAGE 108]. Cover any pimples with HIGHLIGHT.

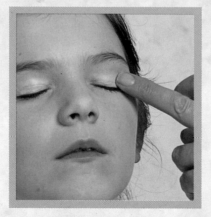

2 Little girls need big eyes, so we have used a very pale cream stick makeup to highlight the eyelids. Blend it over the lids, then POWDER, powdering any pimples you have hidden as well. Define the eyes with a line drawn along the lower eyelashes, using a brown pencil. Don't make it too thick.

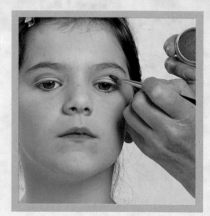

3 On medium to large stages, a socket shadow helps to define the top eyelid. Use a brown powder shadow for white skins and a charcoal one for black skins, working in the same way as you do for caucasian FEMALE makeup.

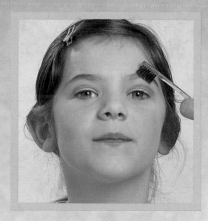

4 Complete the eye makeup with a little mascara. Don't use black mascara unless the hair is naturally black. To make removal easier later, don't use a waterproof type.

5 Brush through the eyebrows to remove any makeup that may be caught in them. If they are quite dark, just apply a little petroleum jelly or color-free mascara to give a shine.

6 If the brows need defining, work some powder shadow through them softly, in a color to match the hair. It is better than pencil or cake for children because it gives soft definition without too sophisticated a shape. Or use block mascara for the eyelashes and the eyebrows.

7 A little ROUGE in the unmade-up position used for men gives a healthy look. Use a pinkish tone on caucasian skins to match any natural warmth, and keep it soft; too much will make the child look flushed. A bright red lipstick on little girls' lips makes them look like dolls, as well as emphasizing the smallness of the natural mouth. Instead, use a pretty peach like this one.

Boys and Ballet Dancers

Here we have a basic make-up for young boys who, obviously, must look natural on stage. The makeup for ballet is also suitable for modern dance and can be adapted for all ages.

See also
☞

○ **Foundation p.13**

○ **Highlighting p.19**

◉ **Powder p.21**

◉ **Rouge p.22**

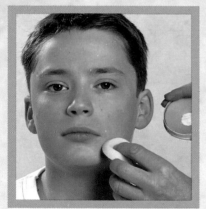

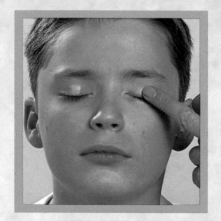

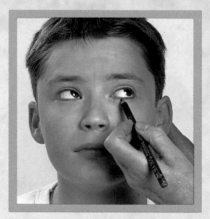

1 Apply a thin wash of cake or creamy cake FOUNDATION and pat dry with a tissue. Be careful not to use too dark a color on caucasian skins; the FEMALE tone is usually a good choice. HISPANIC and DARK SKINS need a matching foundation.

2 If the performance is in a medium or large theater, emphasize the eyes by placing a dot of pale HIGHLIGHT on each eyelid. Blend the highlight quickly over the lids, then POWDER it. If you have chosen a creamy cake, it might be wise to powder the whole face at this point.

3 Ask the child to look up and draw a fine line with a pencil along the roots of the lower lashes. Use brown for white skins, black for darker ones. Very fair eyelashes and eyebrows can be darkened with a little block mascara. If the face needs more color, use a little dry ROUGE in the male position. On caucasian skins use the usual color for women; darker skins need a stronger color.

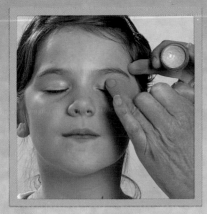  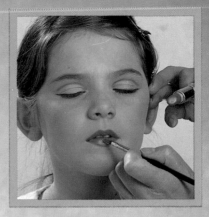

1 For ballet or modern dance use a little more FOUNDATION than in the BASIC MAKEUP, but in the same color. On caucasian skins a soft, pale gray eye shadow gives a good effect without looking bright and over-colored. Darker skins look good with a little lilac shadow. To keep it from being rubbed off, use cream eye shadow and powder it well. On a large stage, add a little shimmer to enlarge the eyes.

2 For dancing the eyes need more emphasis. Draw a top eye line as well as a bottom one with cake or liquid eyeliner, making sure the color matches the hair. Draw a fine line along the lash roots and extend it at the outer corner of the eye without letting it turn up. Mascara the lashes and define the eyebrows.

3 The blusher position for dance shows off the cheekbones, using the same color as the previous makeup. Very small girls should have their ROUGE in the natural position. The lipstick should give clear definition to the lips, but only use red on a really big stage, or it looks precocious on young girls. This picture also gives a good view of the eye makeup.

Planning a Makeup

Planning any special makeup requires care, so give yourself plenty of time to research your character. Find pictures or designs to work from and keep a file of interesting and important faces for future reference. I have chosen one of the 20th century's most famous icons, Marilyn Monroe, to demonstrate the planning process. During her career, her look and hairstyle gradually changed and she looked a little different in each film, but this is probably the most familiar image.

See also

☞

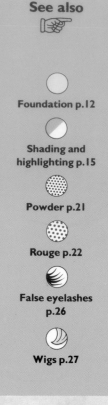

Foundation p.12

Shading and highlighting p.15

Powder p.21

Rouge p.22

False eyelashes p.26

Wigs p.27

Start with an image of your character: a painting, drawing or, preferably, a color photograph. Make a chart of the face from the photograph, showing the facial structure and any strong details

such as eyebrow shape, eye make-up, lips, and in Monroe's case, the beauty spot. I also noted the look of the skin, the type of makeup used, and the false eyelashes.

The hair is an important factor. You may be able to style your own to suit the character, changing the cut and color as appropriate, but a professionally dressed wig makes life a lot easier. When choosing a wig, take the photograph with you so you can discuss the style you want with the supplier.

Check that your ideas do not conflict with those of your director. Then check the costume designs; the colors may affect your make-up choice. For example, if the designer chose a brilliant pink outfit for Marilyn Monroe, her lip and nail color would need to be toned for that scene.

Make sure you have all the make-up and equipment you need, then sit down with your photograph and

chart and practice the makeup. You will find you need to alter your design a little to fit your own face shape. Keep practicing until you feel comfortable with the makeup, wearing it from the technical rehearsal so that by first night you are completely familiar with it.

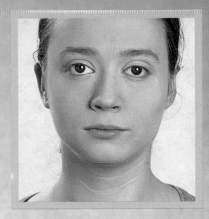

1 Hollywood stars of this period always appeared to have velvety skins. To achieve this look, use a cream stick or, for greasy skins, cake FOUNDATION, applying more, and of a paler color, than usual. Monroe had a short nose, big eyelids, and good cheekbones, so shade under the cheekbones, across the end of the nose, and on the edges of the eye sockets. Adjust the SHADING according to the face shape.

2 Blend the shading, and add HIGHLIGHTS on the eyelids, into the tiredness shadows and on the cheekbones. Highlight down the center of the nose and over the roundness of the end, but not under it. Apply extra highlight, with the face smiling, on the cheeks close to the nose, blending it outward. Soften the highlights carefully, and POWDER well, including the eyelids.

3 Our model has strong lines on her neck which can be hidden with highlight. Paint pale highlight into the lines, powder and then sponge a wash of cake makeup to match the face color over the neck. The skin should now look even and matte, the eyelids large and the cheekbones well-defined.

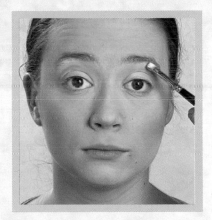

4 Monroe's ROUGE position comes a little closer to the mouth than the basic shape that emphasizes the cheekbones. To help get it in the right position, brush it from in front of the ears (over the shading), up onto the cheekbones and then, with the face smiling, slightly onto the smile. Use a pretty peachy tone.

5 There is no colored eye shadow in this eye makeup, just a pale sheen on the eyelids and under the eyebrows created by powder highlight. Take it over the whole eyelid first, then lift the eyebrows and blend some over the browbone. Don't cover the shader in the socket.

6 Draw a top eye line with brownish-black cake eyeliner or a matte liquid liner, extending it out at the corners in the same way as the CAUCASIAN FEMALE eye line for the medium stage.

7 This eye makeup emphasizes the top lid, so the lower line should be drawn with a softer color, and should not extend beyond the corners – it is more like a male underline. Mascara the top eyelashes only with dark brown – black would be too strong. Then add FALSE EYELASHES, using the half-lashes which go from the center lid to the outer corner. Use natural-looking lashes rather than thick ones.

8 Re-draw the upper eye line to the inner corners to balance the darkness of the false lash roots. Use a little mascara to merge the real and false lashes, and strengthen the socket shadow slightly with a brown powder shader. Brush through the eyebrows and shape them with a dark brown pencil or cake-liner, using your photo for reference. Powder brow makeup will not give the right effect.

9 Marilyn used a beauty spot as part of her look, just to the side of the smile line. Apply it with a dark brown pencil or cake-liner.

10 The lip shape is very important for this makeup. The top lip is curved but not bowed and does not dip strongly in the center, and the shape is over-drawn at the outer corners. To get it right, remembering that this makeup is pre-lip liners, draw the outline with a brown eyebrow pencil.

11 Fill in the lip shape with a soft red or deep peachy lipstick, avoiding modern, muted colors which will look out of period. Soften the pencil line by blending the lipstick into it, blot the lips, and add a little clear lip gloss or petroleum jelly.

12 With the model's own hair color and style, an important part of the look is missing; Marilyn Monroe's blondeness is a vital element of the look.

13 Long hair is always a problem under a wig – if it is put up badly, the head looks an odd shape or enormous. It is best to divide it into sections, roll the pieces into curls, and pin them flat to the skull with bobby pins.

14 When you have pin-curled the whole head, cover the hair for extra security with a stocking cut in half. Knot the cut end and pull the welt over the head, tucking in any stray hairs.

15 Always put on a WIG from the front of the head. If you have a helper, hold the wig front well down on the forehead as they stretch it over the hair. Secure it with bobby pins just above the ears.

16 This wig didn't have a hair-lace front, so to soften the edge and give a widow's peak, we glued a little matching hair onto the forehead. If you are using a hair-lace wig, dab spirit gum under the edge and in front of the ears to secure it.

Losing the Years — Women

This sequence helps you to lose a few years on stage. It works well in medium to large theaters but not, unfortunately, in small venues — the audience is just too close.

See also

Foundation pp.12–13

Shading and highlighting p.15

Powder p.21

Rouge p.22

Wigs p.27

1 The skin changes with age and becomes more transparent, revealing broken capillaries on caucasian skins and patches of darker pigment on black skins. The skin loosens, and this looseness becomes a natural highlight picked up by the lighting and magnifying the age. Use plenty of makeup on the neck and hands. Use cream-colored tooth enamel to brighten yellow teeth, but not if capped.

2 You must use a really good covering foundation, which means cream or cake. Then add all the shadows for the MEDIUM STAGE, but with extra SHADING under the cheekbones, at the sides of the face. This shadow should be softer in color. Add a line of shade along the jaw line from ear to ear, fading it under the jaw and cutting across any sagging skin. Blend all the shading, not forgetting the neck.

3 Add all the basic HIGHLIGHTS, plus a few more that you can see here, to lift out the major lines on the face. Don't get too enthusiastic and try to hide every line — too much highlight will make the face shapeless.

4 Use a pale, matte, cream eye shadow on older eyes, as it doesn't show any crêpe-like skin. Before you POWDER, use cream shader to create the socket shadows; it is easier to blend on loose skin. Do the sockets with the eyes open, or the shadows will disappear when you look ahead. Powder the eyelids thoroughly or the eye shadow will crease.

5 Add ROUGE now or after the eyes are finished. It should be a warm pinkish tone to give a glow to the skin. Take it over the cheekbones, to flatter the face, and over the little area of paleness just where the brush is. If there is a natural highlight (looseness) there, it makes the face look tired.

6 Draw on the eye lines using cake eyeliner, which doesn't drag the skin. Don't make the lines too thick and extend them if you can [SEE PAGES 34–7]. If there are folds across the corners, this may be difficult, so use FALSE EYELASHES. Mascara the lashes and, if necessary, strengthen the socket shadows with powder shader. Define the eyebrows, making sure they are long enough. Add false lashes now.

7 Edge the lips with a dark red or brown pencil and paint a little line of highlight under the bottom lip at the outer corners to sharpen up the shape. Then fill in with a soft pearly red or peachy shade, as in the finished makeup. Finally, add a WIG to suit the coloring.

Losing the Years — Men

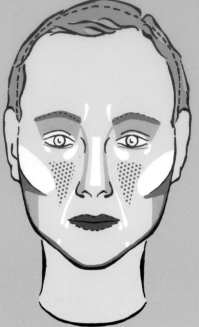

Here is how to make an older man appear younger for a medium to large stage. This makeup is too strong to be believable on a small stage.

See also

Foundation p.13

Shading and highlighting
pp.15, 20

Powder p.21

Rouge p.22

1 The first step is to make the face look healthy and smoother. A slightly tanned FOUNDATION is helpful for caucasian skins – a paler base makes older faces *look* older. Use either cake make-up a little more heavily than usual or a cream base, which will give more cover. Creams are good when you need to make a big jump in age.

2 To make the face look firmer, SHADE and HIGHLIGHT the underlying bone structure. Be sure to cover the loose skin under the eyebrows and along the jaw line, as in the female version of this.

3 Add HIGHLIGHTS to the eyelids, the tiredness shadows under the eyes, the center of the nose, the cheekbones, and along any strong lines that make the face look older. Use the female version of the make-up for guidance. POWDER all over, stretching the skin to get into all the crevices.

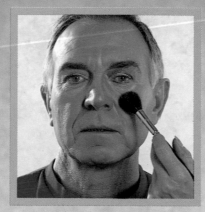

4 Add the usual line under the eyes and mascara the eyelashes top and bottom. Then shape the eyebrows. Start by brushing them up and then brushing the ends down, to help lift the face. Color them with a pencil or liner, working from the center to the outer ends leaving the part close to the nose till last. There, the hair is usually thick and you may not need to do anything to it.

5 Add ROUGE in the usual, natural position, but take care not to cover the highlights disguising the TIREDNESS SHADOWS. If the rouge streaks, you probably haven't powdered well enough so do that area again over the rouge.

6 Older lips may have become thinner – to fill them out, close the mouth and edge it with a brown pencil or, as here, with a brownish-red lining color. If the lips are very pale, you can use a little of this to add warmth, but do not use too much. Finally the hair: you may need to use a wig, but gray hair can be sprayed with a tint that washes out. Don't choose too dark a color, as it is very aging.

7 Use strokes of pencil or cake liner to build up the hairline. You can also use the cake on a sponge to hide small bald patches. Remember to make up the ears, neck, and hands.

Ageing a Middle-aged Face

Sometimes a person in their middle years needs to look older. This sequence shows the effect on a man; a woman would add a little eye shadow and lipstick as appropriate. Adapt the colors as appropriate to dark skins, but leave out the reddening for broken veins on black skin.

See also ☞

Foundation p.12

Shading and highlighting p.15

Powder p.21

Crêpe hair p.25

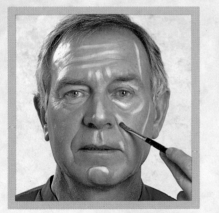

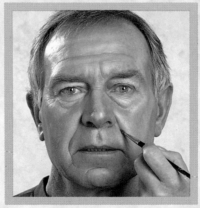

1 For light-skinned people, use a paler FOUNDATION than usual, or no foundation at all. Paler skin looks looser. As the face is already lined, SHADING is only needed to make it look slimmer. HIGHLIGHT the natural folds and lines.

2 Blend the highlights with your finger, taking care they don't creep into the lines or the face will look younger rather than older. Use a small amount of cream shader to deepen the smile lines and tiredness shadows unless they are already quite noticeable.

3 POWDER the whole face well with loose powder, stretching any folds to make sure you set the make-up in them. Make sure the eyelids are really matte. Brush a little spirit gum through the eyebrows to give a wiry look. Don't use too much or you will clog the hairs and create a messy effect.

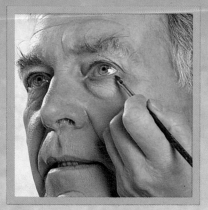

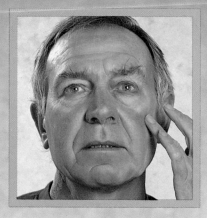

4 Using a fine brush, run a little brownish-red liner under the lower eyelashes and into the outer corners of the eyes, fading the color with your finger, to make the skin there look transparent. Do the same on the eyelids.

5 Stipple red onto the centers of the cheekbones to suggest broken veins. Don't use too much or they will look bruised. Run a little highlight over the glued eyebrow hair with your finger or a toothbrush. Don't use too much.

6 Lips tend to lose their natural warm color as we age, so rub a little highlight over the mouth. It will also help to show up the lines on the lips. It is important to age the neck. Stretch the head up and shade the hollows beside the tendons, then highlight the tendons. Set the neck makeup with loose powder,

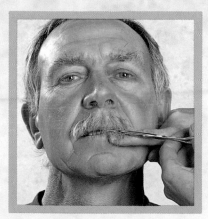

7 A mustache helps to add more age. Here we have used a simple MUSTACHE made with crêpe wool laid onto spirit gum. When the whole mustache has been applied, trim it to the right length, working step by step to avoid cutting off too much. You can fix the finished mustache with a fixing gel or acrylic spray; cover the eyes and nostrils while doing this.

Adding Age – Women

This three-stage sequence demonstrates the principles of aging on a 24-year-old woman. We will be adding 20 years at each stage, starting with a 35-year-old in the 1950s. Applied crudely, in the final stages this makeup could look like a caricature, and it is better to look too young than to overdo the aging.

See also ☞

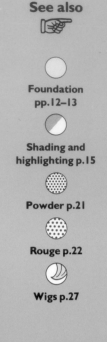

Foundation pp.12–13

Shading and highlighting p.15

Powder p.21

Rouge p.22

Wigs p.27

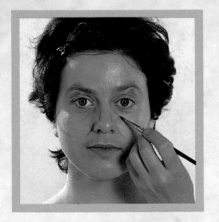

1 Begin with a straight makeup FOUNDATION and put on all the SHADING needed to improve the face. Drop the chin and look in a mirror, to trace in the tiredness shadows and the smile lines. Don't make them too long or the face will look sad.

2 Blend the shadows and run a finger or sponge tip down the age lines to soften them. Apply the HIGHLIGHTS as shown and blend them. There should be a noticeable paleness. POWDER the face.

3 After powdering, the face should look like this. The lines are wear lines from the movement of the mouth and eyes. For an unmade-up look, add highlight on the eyelids at this stage, and powder it.

4 The fashionable makeup used green eye shadow and created doe eyes. Emphasize the top line with dark brown or black eyeliner, and use a dark brown powder shadow to draw a softer bottom line. Do the socket line in the usual way, and mascara only the top lashes. The eyebrows should be shortish and quite angular. Omit the colored eye shadow and soften the eye lines to give a more natural look.

5 Apply blusher to the points of the cheekbones only, or, for an unmade-up look, use the natural position in the ROUGE SECTION, and a softer color.

6 Use a coral-toned lipstick and paint the shape with a pointed top lip. For a natural mouth use a soft muted peach tone. For a character set in another period, check on the right styles of the time, for example, the 1940s or 1960s.

7 Dress the hair for the period or use an appropriate WIG. If the dress is low-cut, make up all the skin that shows as well, following the advice in BODY MAKEUP.

The Middle Years

It is now the 1970s and our character is 55 years old and an avid gardener.

1 Use a male FOUNDATION to give a light tan. Include the neck and hands. Apply all the SHADING for the previous stage except those on the browbone. Don't shade for slimness. Shade the temples, the hollow under the nose, the corners of the mouth, under the mouth, and the centre of the chin. Draw shadows each side of the jaw, and trace broken lines on the neck in the natural creases.

2 Shade the temples in a line from the eyebrows to the hairline and back to the sides of the face. Press the skin at the sides of the mouth in for those areas. Center the shadow to loosen the jaw line in the crease on the point of the chin, unless you have a long chin, and below the lines at the corners of the mouth. Press the skin of the browbone in; shade inside the resulting fold, next to the nose.

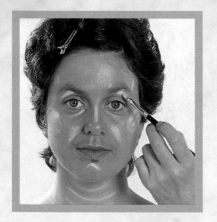

3 Blend the shading and, using a brush for precision, add the highlights from the previous make-up, plus the extra ones shown. Highlight gives realism, and each one does a different job for the shadow it complements. Add neck makeup over the age lines. They will show, so take care to powder them well.

4 After powdering, you can see that the highlights add to the hollowing of the temples, create folds under the eyebrows, and make the skin under the eyes appear soft and lined. The smile lines are much deeper, the jaw line looser, and the neck older. Powder carefully – any shine will spoil the effect.

5 Strengthen the edges of the eye folds, the tired shadows, and the smile lines by edging them with pencil after powdering. After drawing them, run a finger along them to make them seem like part of the structure.

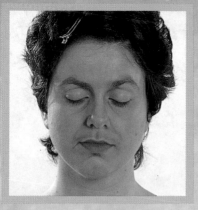

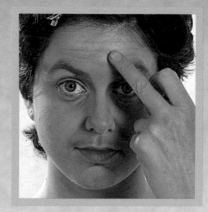

6 With the eyes closed, you can see the strengthened lines and the shading.

7 To age a forehead, don't simply lift the eyebrows and draw in every line. Raise the eyebrows and run a little highlight over the furrows with your finger. If they are quite deep when the eyebrows are relaxed, the face lines will appear. If this doesn't work, trace two rows of broken lines into a couple of natural ones and fade them, making sure there are broad highlights above and below each line.

8 Apply the ROUGE in a v-shape on the center of the cheek. Don't go over the highlights for the smile lines. Use highlight as eye shadow for small eyelids; otherwise, leave the eyelids alone. Draw top eye lines with extensions for medium-sized stages, and lower lines, but make sure they don't look like age lines under the eyes. Mascara the lashes, shape the eyebrows, and use a soft peachy lip color.

9 You can add small amounts of very realistic gray to dark hair by taking a little highlight on your finger and stroking it up the hair. Men can do this at the sides of the hair and on beards and mustaches.

Old Age

It is now the 1990s and our woman is in her seventies. It is a makeup for distance.

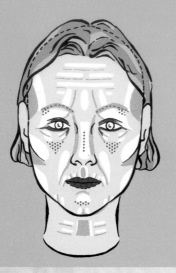

1 This requires a WIG, so cover the hair securely. You can buy special nets, but the top of a stocking with the foot cut off and a knot tied on the top of the head is just as good. To make the eyebrows look sparse, brush a little spirit gum inward through the hairs. Only use a little, or you will get lumps, and work quickly before the gum dries. Work on one eyebrow at a time.

2 Use a FOUNDATION two shades paler than normal, and apply it thinly. Add all the shadows for the middle years, extending some lines and adding an extra one under the eyes to suggest bags. Age the neck by stretching it up, sucking in hard under the chin, and SHADING the hollows between the tendons. On a man, shade under the Adam's apple. Draw a line to emphasize any plumpness under the chin.

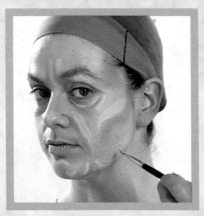

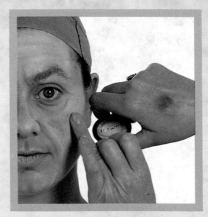

3 On the completed shading, you can see the new line under the eyes, curving down from the outer corner and along the point of the cheekbone, but it does not join up with the tiredness shadow. The cheek shading has dropped down slightly from the end of the cheekbone toward the mouth to give a skull-like shape. The smile lines are longer, and the curve of the chin has been drawn in.

4 Add extra HIGHLIGHTS under the eyes and on the chin. The cheekbone highlights follow the shading and the neck tendons have been emphasized. The line at the mouth corner has been drawn up a little; highlight on the lips shows up the natural lines. Frown lines are drawn from out of the eyebrows and up into the natural creases. Pull the brows together to find them. Blend the highlights carefully.

5 POWDER very carefully. For stronger lines, take a pencil or a little cake-liner on a brush and deepen the bags, frown lines, eye folds, and the smile shading. Fade the new lines with your finger; add a little more highlight at the top of the eye folds and slightly away from the smile lines. Re-powder. Stipple ROUGE onto the cheeks. Use brownish-red cream liner.

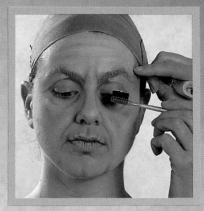

6 Run Kryolan EF9 cream liner along the inner rim of the eyes to make them look watery. Wearers of contact lenses or those with sensitive eyes should skip this step.

7 Purse the mouth and trace in four of the lines on the top lip, two on each side above the edge, with a soft brown pencil or a brownish-red lining color. Relax the mouth and trace in five lines on the lower lip, including the central one, but don't draw them down to the edge. Highlight between the lines. On the top lip take it a little higher than the shadows.

8 Draw a few stray hairs at the inner ends of the eyebrows in the same position and at the same angle as the natural ones. Gray the eyebrows with a little highlight, working toward the nose. Lightly paint a few highlight hairs among those you drew. Real eyelashes don't go gray, but here it helps to whiten them. Mascara the lashes with a little highlight on a small toothbrush. Now put on the WIG.

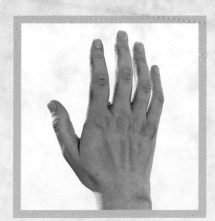

9 To age the hands, apply the foundation as for BODY MAKEUP, then add the shadows in the picture, laying the hands on a flat surface. To find the tendons, press the palms down and lift the fingers. Blend the shadows and add the highlights as shown, clenching the hand into a fist to show the knuckles clearly. Soften the highlights and powder the hands.

Degeneration

This routine shows the gradual changes in a young man, from fresh-faced health to a down-and-out living rough. The stages contain a number of effects which can be incorporated into other characters. The redness doesn't work on really dark skins, so forget broken veins and use a black liner for the tiredness shadows.

See also
☞

Highlighting p.15

Powder p.21

Crêpe hair p.25

STAGE ONE
We are beginning with a healthy young man, so use a basic straight makeup appropriate to the stage size [SEE PAGES 44–49]. Highlight out natural dark shadows under the eyes [SEE PAGE 14].

STAGE TWO
Drop the chin and paint a little brownish-red liner into the natural shadows, onto the eyelids, and at the outer corners of the eyes. Trace some a little way along the smile lines and soften it. Add HIGHLIGHTS in a triangle between the eyes and the tiredness shadows to look like bags. Add a broad line on the cheeks close to the smile lines. Blend and POWDER.

STAGE THREE
1 Now our character doesn't shave regularly, so we add beard shadow. Use cake makeup or cake eyeliner; brownish-black for caucasian skins, black for really dark ones, stippling it over the chin and upper lip with a slightly damp sponge. It is easy to apply and you can wipe it off quickly by taking a sponge and applying flesh-colored cake over it.

2 Run a little more red under the eyes and stipple it onto the cheeks, taking care not to cover the highlight. Draw a second line under the eyes, leaving a gap between them, to increase the bags. Trace frown lines above the nose, curving into the eyebrows, and draw lines down at the corners of the mouth. Fade them all slightly. Add more highlights, blend carefully (don't cover the lines), and powder.

STAGE FOUR

1 The character now has heavy beard shadow and it needs to show as hair growing. Use chopped-up crêpe hair or wool, prepared as shown in USING BEARDS. Paint spirit gum over the beard shadow, press a slightly damp sponge onto the crêpe pieces, and apply them to the gummed area. Add as much as you need, remembering to cover under the chin as well.

2 Our model has two old scars on his forehead. To use them as part of the character, paint brownish-red liner into the indentations to make them look newer, and add a soft amount of the same color around the scars to suggest sore skin. You can do the same thing on an unscarred forehead. Press on a little powder to set the scars and add more scars as needed.

3 Finally, paint a red line on the inner rim of the eyes to make them look bloodshot. Use Kryolan EF9 Supracolor for this, as it doesn't irritate the eyes, but don't use it with contact lenses or sensitive eyes. Dirty the hair by putting grease on it and rubbing a little talc through it. Dirty skin is created with cake liner.

STAGE TWO

Tiredness is now beginning to show in the character. As this makeup builds up gradually, you can adjust it to suit the degrees of degeneration.

STAGE THREE

This beard shadow created from makeup is especially versatile in quick-change scenes; simply wipe it off and reapply a foundation.

STAGE FOUR

Think of what real men living on the streets look like. Here the effect is enhanced by dirty, disheveled hair. You could also add cuts, bruising, or a black eye if the character is having a very hard time.

Town and Country Girl

Based on the caucasian female makeup, one character is a fresh-faced, innocent girl with plump apple cheeks and freckles. The other is the glossy, over made-up glamour girl often seen with successful men.

See also

Foundation p.12

Shading and highlighting p.15

Powder p.21

Rouge p.22

1 Begin with a caucasian female FOUNDATION color, or make the character very tanned – either choice works well. SHADE and HIGHLIGHT to improve the facial structure and be sure to hide any tiredness shadows. POWDER with translucent powder. Apply a white or cream powder shimmer from the eyelashes to the eyebrows.

2 Line the eyes with black liquid eyeliner, keeping the line narrow and extending the outer corners as in a straight makeup, but drawing right round the inner corners. Feather a little pale powder brown over the lids, leaving the centers white, or use pink or peach eye shadow. Define the eye socket with a dark brown powder shadow, fading it onto the outer edge of the eyelid.

3 Add iridescent powder shimmer to the eyelid center and under the brow. Apply at least two layers of black mascara and brush through the lashes. Use a brownish ROUGE in the hollows under the cheekbones and up over the temples. Outline the lips with dark red, filling in with a medium-toned color. Take a line of highlight under the outer corners of the lower lip, and powder. Finish with a WIG with tints and volume.

1 To suggest healthy-looking skin, choose a caucasian, not too pale, FOUNDATION. SHADE and HIGHLIGHT the eye area only (unless you are shaping a naturally broad face or large nose), using the highlight as eye shadow, then smile and paint highlight onto the fatness of the smile, blending it into a soft round shape.

2 Add top and bottom eye lines and socket shadows, and mascara the eyelashes. Brush through and color the eyebrows; add a little petroleum jelly to unplucked brows and hair-like strokes to thin brows with a pencil or cake liner, following the natural hairs. Draw some freckles on with a sharp brown pencil across the nose, on the cheeks close to it, and on the forehead; pat them carefully.

3 The lips need to look natural, so choose a peachy tone; on a small stage you may need no lipstick. Finally, add ROUGE, using a warm rosy shade with no blue in it. Take it onto the fatness of the smile, but leave an area of pale highlight around it; this is a happy face.

Urban and Country Man

This characterization contrasts a stereotype city dweller with his rural counterpart. Our first character probably works for a large corporation, and is ambitious and ruthless. The country gentleman works perhaps as a farmer, and life and the weather have aged him more.

See also ☞

Foundation p.13

Shading and highlighting p.15

Powder p.21

Rouge p.22

1 Apply a caucasian FOUNDATION color and SHADE under the cheekbones and down the sides of the nose. Add the HIGHLIGHTS on the cheekbones and down the center of the nose. Shade the brow bones, unless the eyebrows are heavy, and take a little around the inner corners of the eyes. Highlight one eyelid, preferably the one that is naturally bigger, and POWDER the whole face.

2 Using a pencil or a cake liner and brush, bring the eyebrows nearer to the nose, working up with small strokes. If you are using cake liner, check the color on the back of your hand before you start. If you use a pencil, keep wiping the point on a tissue as you go to remove any powder. Line under the eye as usual and mascara only the top lashes.

3 Using a basic male color, apply the ROUGE, slightly higher than usual and along the cheekbones, but not as far as the hairline. This adds to the lean look. Darken the lips slightly with a little brownish-red lip liner on a finger or brush. Don't use too much color and don't go over the edge of the lips. If the mouth is large and well colored, leave out this step.

1 Start with a tanned FOUNDATION applied thinly. SHADE and HIGHLIGHT the eyes, drop the chin and trace shader into the tiredness lines under the eyes, the smile lines and the lines at the corners of the mouth. Add highlights between the tiredness shadows and the eyes and on the cheek sides of the smile lines. Make sure none of the highlight looks thin and striped. Blend, and POWDER carefully.

2 Underline the eyes as for a caucasian makeup and apply a little mascara. Then brush powder blusher in the color you use normally across the forehead close to the hairline, down the center of the nose and near the natural position for men [SEE PAGE 22], but a little closer to the middle of the cheeks. On a small stage, leave out the eye lines and mascara.

3 Stipple a little brownish-red cream liner over the rouge and on the neck and chin with a finger or stipple sponge. Do not use too much or it will look like bruising. Build the eyebrow shape with a pencil or cake liner, working among the natural hairs to make the brows look heavier. Leave the lips natural.

Period Makeup – The 1940s

Women of this period wore either very little makeup – powder, rouge, and lipstick – or they wore a lot. A velvety matte skin, arched eyebrows, and a distinctive lip shape are key elements of the look. Panstick and pancake were used extensively for day makeup. The hairstyle is typical of this period.

See also

Restoration period p.80

Foundation p.12

Shading and highlighting p.15

Powder p.21

False eyelashes p.26

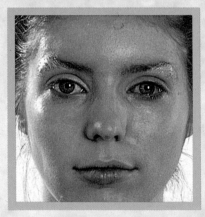

1 Thick eyebrows are blocked out or, as here, partly blocked out, as explained in detail in the RESTORATION FOP MAKEUP. Then apply either a stick or cake FOUNDATION – it should be absolutely smooth and should look madeup. You may need to apply it on a brush where you blocked out the eyebrows. Choose a pale tone unless the skin is naturally dark.

2 If you used a cake foundation, you will need a compressed powder which has a built-in foundation. SHADE and HIGHLIGHT as usual, but unless the eyes are deep set, leave out the shading on the browbones. Highlight the eyelids strongly and POWDER heavily with a matte, pale powder. You can use translucent, but it has a sheen.

3 The eyebrow is arched strongly with a very sharp pencil or cake eyeliner – brownish-black is best. Creating thin brows that match is difficult, but if you do the harder side first, it will be a lot easier. If you get the line too thick, paint over it with a little foundation or highlight, and powder.

4 Outline the eyes in the same way as for caucasian makeup and be sure to make a good socket shadow to compensate for no shading on the browbone. In the 1940s, some women used petroleum jelly on their eyelids, which caught the light and made the eyes look bigger; you can re-create that with a little shimmer to make the lids appear shiny.

5 Mascara the top lashes and brush through them to separate the hairs. Leave the bottom lashes; in the 1940s they didn't mascara them. A pair of spindly EYELASHES will help this look, but thick ones would ruin it. Trim the inner corners, but keep the lashes long.

6 Apply the ROUGE as a triangle of color on the center of the cheekbones. You will find this easier to do with a piece of cotton than with a brush. The color should tone with the lipstick and be a shade of red, coral, or pink, as there were no brownish-pink rouges available at that time.

7 Lips had a very distinctive rounded shape in the 1940s, influenced by the Hollywood stars. If your character is really tough, try this shape, favored by Joan Crawford. Scarlet, deep rosy reds, and tangerines were popular lipstick colors. Finally, add a beauty spot in black pencil on the cheekbone.

The 1960s

See also ☞

The key features for the high-fashion look for this time are the rouge position, false eyelashes, and heavy eyelids. Tans were fashionable, so a deeper foundation might be appropriate, depending on the time of year in the production. Otherwise, stick to your usual color. Add the shadows and highlights for caucasian makeup.

Foundation p.12

Shading and highlighting p.15

Rouge p.22

False eyelashes p.26

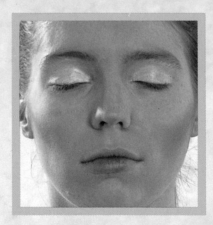

1 Start with a basic FOUNDATION, and straight SHADING and HIGHLIGHTING. The rouge position changed and browner tones became fashionable. Choose one like a shading but with a touch of pink in it. Suck in the cheeks and apply the ROUGE in the hollows where the shading has been applied. The cheekbones should not be rouged at all, merely underneath them. It should look quite dark.

2 White was the most fashionable eye shadow. You can reproduce it with a white, pearlized powder shadow, or a white cream lining color. Take the color over the whole area from eyebrows to eyelashes. Black eyeliner was the fashion, but for very fair lashes dark brown gives a strong enough effect. Women used stage eye lines in their ordinary makeup, but with a stronger socket shadow.

3 The model Twiggy started a popular fashion for lashes drawn under the eyes with cake eyeliner rather than using an underline. Be careful not to make them too long close to the nose, and draw them at the same angle as your own. See the next step for more detail. Mistakes can be painted out with a little highlight. See how huge this eye is beginning to look.

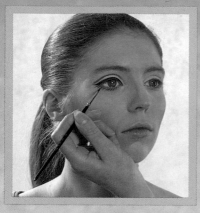

4 The eyebrows were softly defined, but not as important or as stylized as the eyes. Improve the shape to frame the eye if necessary, but keep it natural. The effect is one of high drama on the eyes. Although some women used thicker eye lines than these, they close up the eyes on stage and therefore aren't advisable unless you are very close to the audience.

5 Trim FALSE LASHES to make the tips a little shaggy and shorten the hairs at the inner corners so they don't pull the eyes together. Make sure the eyelid is matte, and mascara the eyelashes before putting on the false ones. When the false lashes are in place, push the eyelid down a little to cover the strip they are attached to, then redraw the top eye line to even up the edge.

6 Darken the socket shadow further. The Brigitte Bardot fashion for outlining the lips with a darker color, or a brown pencil, remained popular. The shape began to lift toward the outer corners in contrast to the more pointed 1950s lips.

7 Lip colors varied between pale, chalky colors and peachy tones, but strong reds were out. Lip gloss became big news, and in fashion photography cod-liver oil was used to give really shiny mouths. The finished face should look highly made up and very glamorous.

The Restoration

The Restoration period was a time of licentious lifestyles. The fashion was for elaborate, stylized makeup, and here we recreate the highly colored yet fragile "Dresden doll" look of a fashionable lady; but first, the most extreme makeup of all, worn by fops. These effects look wonderful in full costume.

See also ☞

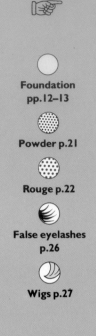

Foundation pp.12–13

Powder p.21

Rouge p.22

False eyelashes p.26

Wigs p.27

1 Before beginning the makeup, you must block out the eyebrows. Start by brushing spirit gum through them, working toward the nose. Work quickly before it dries.

2 With a child's toothbrush or large, clean mascara brush, brush the hairs up as hard as you can, flattening them to the face. Roll a long brush handle up the hairs while they dry, making sure every hair is glued down.

3 Mortician's wax, such as Naturo Plastic or Special Plastic, is best for blocking out. It comes in soft and firm textures, the former being more difficult to use with hot hands. Using a clay modeling tool, dig out a little wax and smooth it on the back of your hand, then scoop up a small amount and smear it over the eyebrow. Cover the hairs with a thin layer to give a smooth surface.

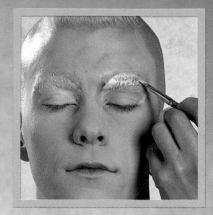

4 Seal the wax after applying it with liquid latex or a clear film called Sealor, covering the brows and overlapping slightly onto the surrounding skin. Let it dry before you proceed. Using a finger to apply the sealant saves the bother of cleaning brushes.

5 Fops used powdered white lead to give a flat, white skin. This pale highlight will look white on stage without being harsh. You can use cream or, as here, a creamy cake makeup. Apply it heavily, taking it over the wax. With black skin, leave out this pale FOUNDATION as it will make the skin look gray. Change the other colors to match the skin tone.

6 Use light blue eye shadow for a strong period feel, or just brush on cream highlight. Lilac is better for black skin. Paint an arched shape covering the eyebrows and going right down to the eyelashes. The better you draw the shape over the brows, the easier it will be to do the new eyebrows later.

7 POWDER lavishly, paying particular attention to the eye shadow – it must be set well or it will become greasy and settle into blue lines. Use translucent powder or even unperfumed talcum. When you have finished, the skin must look matte and powdery; if it doesn't, powder again.

8 Creating the high, arched, thin, black eyebrows is difficult. Use a really sharp pencil, or cake liner and a good brush, to draw the shape along the edge of the eye shadow. Balance your little finger on the cheek to keep your hand steady. Dot the lines on first, matching the two brows before filling them in.

9 Don't worry if the eyebrows are slightly different in shape. Line the lower eyelids as you would for a CAUCASIAN MAKEUP, using dark brown eyeliner, then mascara the eyelashes with dark brown.

10 Use a small cotton ball to apply brightly colored high spots of ROUGE in tight little circles of red on the points of the cheekbones. It should look strong. If the shape becomes larger than you intended, reduce it with highlight and try again.

11 Patches were very fashionable in the Restoration years. Originally used to hide scarring from smallpox, they developed into fashion accessories with a hidden language. Made of flock, the shapes included the symbols of playing cards, stars, moons, and even coaches and horses. Paint them on with black cake eyeliner or a sharp black pencil.

12 The lipstick should be the brightest scarlet you can find, and the shape a tiny bow. Paint out naturally strong-colored lips before drawing the new shape.

13 It is only when you get the costume and WIG on that you see the full effect of this extra-ordinary makeup. This tall wig is awkward to handle, so fit it carefully [SEE PAGE 27], taking care not to smudge the makeup.

1 Block out all except very thin and fair eyebrows, as in the FOP makeup. Here we only needed to hide half the eyebrows. Then cover the whole face with very pale cream stick FOUNDATION, or cake makeup for greasy skins, using a brush to paint it over the waxed brows. POWDER lavishly, except on the eyelids and browbones.

2 Paint pale blue or pale lilac cream shadow or lining color from the roots of the eyelashes to where the new eyebrows will be, covering the waxed area as well. You may need to make the color a little whiter over the wax. Powder the shadow carefully to set it. Don't worry if the blocked eyebrows still show a little; they won't when the new ones are added.

3 Draw arched eyebrows as before. They must be thin but clearly defined, in a soft arch for sweet ladies and more angled for spiteful ones. The eye makeup is similar to that for CAUCASIAN MAKEUP, but without shading; use brown for the eye lines and socket shadows.

4 Apply a brilliant but soft pink ROUGE, unless the costume is yellow or orange (then use a soft red), in two spots on the cheek-bones. Balance the patches or beauty spots, using one on a cheekbone and something else, for example a heart shape, near the mouth on the opposite side. Lips are little cupid's bows of bright red. Add rouge to the fullness of the breasts, and an extra patch.

Animal Makeup – Lion

See also

For this type of makeup, you must have front and side color reference photographs of the real animal to work from, showing the coloring, the lie of the hair, and the shape of the nose, mouth, and eyes. Do a rough chart of these major features, and refer to the chart and photographs while working. For the makeup to work, disguise the nose and mouth.

Restoration p.80

Foundation p.13

Shading and highlighting p.15

False hair p.24

False eyelashes p.26

Wigs p.27

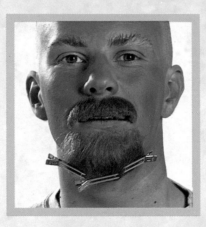

1 Start by disguising the eyebrows – especially if they are dark and bushy – using the spirit-gum method [SEE RESTORATION], but without the wax stage, as the raised hairs will become part of the fur later. The basic FOUNDATION color will vary according to the mane and costume. It is best to use a creamy, self-setting CAKE FOUNDATION. Our lion is wearing a dark olive tan cake.

2 A full MUSTACHE and a small BEARD help a male lion make-up, and should be glued on now. The beard we used was rather straight, so we sprayed it with gel and pinned it up to set it in a more rounded shape.

3 Using a dark brown eyebrow pencil with a good point, trace in the eye shape and the lion nose, making sure the nose covers the end of the actor's own nose. Doing these now makes the rest of the design easier.

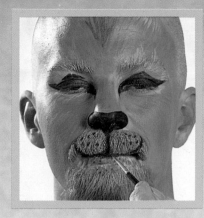

4 Use a palette of creamy cake makeup called Aquacolors to draw the fur in shades of brown and white. The makeup is like watercolor paint. Roughly sketch in the large areas of dark brown, including a v-shape on the forehead, then paint on the white around the eyes and on the beard and mustache. Draw fine strokes of white up through the glued eyebrows and onto the forehead.

5 Draw in the eye shape with black. Go around the inner corner and drop the line down toward the nose, fading it at the end, and angling the outer corners upward. Cover the whole eyelid, rising to a point in the center. Color in the end of the nose, taking the black around the nostrils and down in a straight line onto the mustache. Curve it away on both sides and dot black on the white area of the mustache.

6 Darken the lower part of the beard to make it recede. Take care to keep the rounded shape of the white area. Darken the lower lip with a little gray-brown mix. Check the photograph to see how you are doing and step back to check the audience's view.

7 Add two larger lines of SHADING up from the center of the eyebrows, shaping to give high cheekbones and folds down the sides of the muzzle. Darken the sides of the mustache, and edge the white of the beard with black. Stroke very dark brown on the cheeks, under the eyes, and down the neck, and soften the vee on the forehead with strokes of white and brown. Finally, add the WIG.

Fantasy Makeup – Titania

This famous Shakespearean character from A Midsummer Night's Dream has been interpreted in many different ways over the years. Our fairy queen is young and willful, a pale green woodland creature with huge silvery eyes. Cover every bit of skin that shows with the green makeup, as any uncovered areas will look very pink.

See also ☞

Foundation p.12

Shading and highlighting p.15

Powder p.21

False eyelashes p.26

Restoration p.80

1 Brush the hair tight to the head and as high as you can get it. Use 2-inch Leukoflex tape to create huge new eyelids. Make a template of the new eyelid shape by laying tracing paper across the closed lid and tracing on the new shape with a pencil. It is important that the false lids fit comfortably.

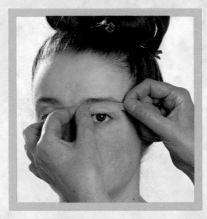

2 Cut out two templates, reversing one to give a left and a right, and mark them L and R. Stick them to the adhesive side of the tape, then cut them out and peel off the Leukoflex. Tone the face, and when the eyelids are dry, position a false lid over the natural one with the eye open, gently stretching the skin out and up toward the eyebrow end.

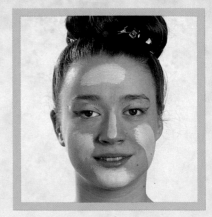

3 When both lids are in position, the eyes should be slanted but not over-stretched, and should feel comfortable. Trace in the corner extensions to see how the shapes work. Apply a pale green FOUNDATION – this one is called Blithe Spirit, created for the ghost of Elvira in Noel Coward's play, and it comes in cake, cream stick and fluid forms. Blend the color to a smooth, even greenness.

4 For pretty makeups in unusual colors, SHADING in a darker version of the base tone looks good. All the shadows need to be exaggerated because this is a stylized makeup, but any on the nose should be softer than the rest or it will dominate the face. We have exaggerated the crease of the chin to suggest determination.

5 White HIGHLIGHTS emphasize the cheekbones, center nose and chin, and hide the tiredness shadows. Paint a strong amount of white on the new eyelid shapes and POWDER the whole face with talcum or a very pale translucent powder – in some brands, translucent is sold as white. Blend iridescent white shimmer over the eyelids to give a silvery effect.

6 Using black liner, edge the top eyelid, lifting the extension to follow the new shape right down and slightly beyond the inner corner. Take the lower line wider under the inner corner, and draw an exaggerated socket shadow covering the top edge of the tape. Mascara well. Add FALSE EYELASHES from the lid center to beyond the ends. Paint a little white between the eye lines at the corners.

7 Draw angled black eyebrows, flicking up the corners to follow the shading. Heavy brows should be partly or wholly blocked out [SEE RESTORATION]. This purplish-blue lip color works well with the greens. Edge the mouth with a darker version of the blue, made by mixing in a little black. Finally, extend the nostrils using black cake eyeliner or grease liner. If you use grease, don't forget to powder.

Special Effects

See also

Foundation p.12

Shading and
highlighting p.15

Powder p.21

Blood p.123

Here are some simple techniques that look totally realistic for theater, and also work for film and TV. In addition to the range of makeup already used, these techniques use mortician's wax or putty, rigid collodion, and Leukoflex tape. Always think of what you want to create first and position the wax or putty on a non-movable part of the face (like the bridge of the nose), or it will fall off. Collodion is good for creating old scars and thin, deep cuts, but only works on loose skin. Never use it close to the eyes or on sensitive or broken skin.

SIMPLE CUTS

1 Powder the skin to remove shine and stickiness; otherwise, the colors will smear. It is also easier to stipple on a dry surface. Dab a little EF9 liner on the back of your hand to ensure you don't use too much. You only need a smear of red for the pale pink soreness around a cut. Stipple a line on the face in the appropriate position.

2 Using the same color and the wooden point of a brush handle, dig a little dark red out of the jar and dab it down the center of the pale red. It needs to be quite thick in texture.

3 A cut caused by a sharp instrument will be thin at the ends and wider in the center. To make the surrounding skin look swollen, take a little more of the lighter color and run two curved lines of it a little way from the cut, as shown.

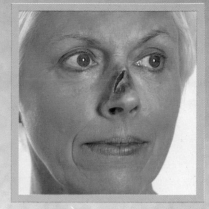

COMPLEX CUTS

1 Apply FOUNDATION, POWDER the nose, and if the cut is to stay on for some time, use the spirit gum and cotton technique [PAGE 91]. Roll a piece of wax into a sausage shape and press this onto the nose. Press the edges down, using the flat end of the tool, and holding the wax with your hand. The edges must be absolutely flat or the light will cast a shadow around the cut.

2 When the wax is secure and smooth, very carefully cut through the center of the shape, taking great care not to cut the skin. If you use the cutter again, wipe it on a tissue, because it could lift the wax if it is too sticky. Seal the cut with latex or Sealor, smoothing it over the wax and surrounding area.

3 Redden around the new cut to add authenticity in the same way as for the SIMPLE CUT, but on the wax itself, using a small brush rather than your finger. Paint dark red thickly into the cut, mixing in a little petroleum jelly for a wet look. Notice how the edge of the wax is left uncolored, making a highlight around it, which is particularly important on a large stage.

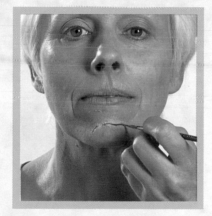

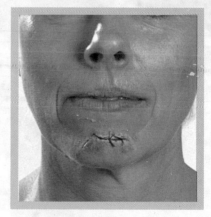

CUT WITH STITCHES

1 For a lasting effect, apply spirit gum and cotton as shown in the WAX NOSE technique [SEE PAGE 91]. Then roll a small amount of wax into a thin sausage, flatten it, and press it onto the chin, keeping hold of it while you press around the edges to secure it. Smooth the edges to fade the wax into the skin.

2 Carefully cut through the wax with a sharp instrument, making a long, thin scar. If you work straight along the center, it will look like a slit, and if you cut closer to the bottom, it will look like a flap of skin. Using a fine brush, paint dark red liner into the cut. A recent injury will also have some redness and soreness around it.

3 To make the stitches, tie knots in some black button thread and cut it to leave two tails for each knot. Carefully press the knots onto the cut. If they fall off, dab a little eyelash adhesive on them.

CUT THROAT

1 Create the effect of dead skin with highlight or a gray-green Kryolan color called 1742. Apply it thinly, then powder the neck. Paint a line of collodion across the throat; you may need to do this twice. As it dries it tightens the skin, forming a scar. The effect can be seen after a few minutes.

2 Color the cut with a dark red to give it depth, using a brownish rather than a bluish tone. We've used EF9, which is probably the best one for special effects, but you can mix a gray-brown with a bright red for a similar effect.

3 For even more depth, take a little of the same color on a finger and, leaving a gap, redden the skin above and below the gash. You need only a smear of color. Then add blood, running from the center – the most open part. Some situations need more blood than others, but it is usually better to use a small amount and show the cut clearly for a more horrific effect.

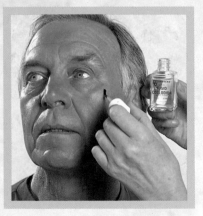

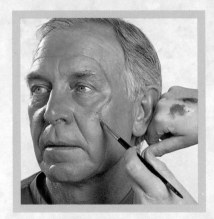

COLLODION SCARS

1 Paint the collodion onto the face with the brush provided, adding a second layer if necessary. When the collodion dries it contracts, pulling the skin into a scar. It will look shiny and need covering with makeup.

2 Paint over the collodion with a mixture of red, brown, and yellow lining colors, being sure to cover any shiny areas. For medium to large stages, HIGHLIGHT around the scar to give it more depth, taking care not to catch any on the edge of the collodion.

3 POWDER the whole area well. When the collodion has been on for some time, the edges will begin to lift, but the scar will not fall off.

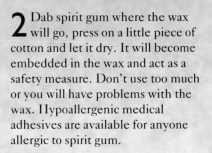

WAX NOSE

1 Wax will create bumps and fatten the end of the nose, but it won't lengthen it successfully. You cannot use it between the eyebrows, or on any other part that moves; it will fall off. So choose the position carefully, then put on the FOUNDATION and set it, making it easier to match the nose color to the skin later.

2 Dab spirit gum where the wax will go, press on a little piece of cotton and let it dry. It will become embedded in the wax and act as a safety measure. Don't use too much or you will have problems with the wax. Hypoallergenic medical adhesives are available for anyone allergic to spirit gum.

3 Using a clay modeling tool, dig out a small piece of wax and roll it into a ball, working quickly if you have hot hands. Flatten the ball and place it on the cotton. Shaping the wax needs patience; always hold it with one hand while smoothing down the edges with the modeling tool, or it may come off. When happy with the front view, check both sides in the mirror.

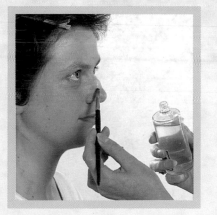

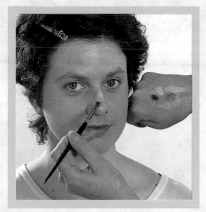

4 Nothing is guaranteed to hold the nose on in all circumstances, but one way of making it more secure is to paint a layer or two of liquid latex over the whole nose. Another is to seal it with a product called Sealor. Either way, if the nose gets squashed, you will have to start again.

5 Coloring the wax is often the hardest part. You need a cream makeup, and usually more than one color. On caucasian skins, this can mean a base tone, highlight, and a little red. Experiment to find which mixture works best, but be careful the nose doesn't turn gray. When you have finished, press on a lot of powder and brush off the excess.

6 Aim for a lump to suit the size of the nose; too big a piece of wax will sit like a saddle and look odd. You can always add more if needed. Similarly, a small bump on a large nose will also look strange. Nose putty is firmer and more difficult to use than wax, but is better if you have hot hands. Never use grease to soften the edges of putty; a damp finger works best.

Black and Distorted Eye

It isn't difficult to create a black eye or a damaged eye that looks totally genuine, even for small-stage work where you are nose to nose with your audience. As usual, think about what you want to achieve, and use reference pictures if necessary.

BLACK EYE

1 Begin by HIGHLIGHTING around one eye – if one naturally looks smaller than the other, choose that one. The highlight will make the eye look smaller and puffier.

2 Blend the highlight and POWDER well. To give a really powerful contrast, SHADE and HIGHLIGHT the other eye normally.

3 Using dark red cream liner on a brush, draw a line under the eye and into the outer corner. Fade the color to soften it.

4 Now work a little brownish-red liner onto your other hand and stipple color under the outer corner of the eye, on the eyelid and browbone, and on the bone above the end of the eyebrow. Don't join the areas or it will look like a pattern. Then draw in the tiredness shadow.

5 To make the eye look bruised, add a little purple or blue liner over the red; too much will spoil the effect. For a bloodshot look, run a little Kryolan EF9 liner along the inner rim of the lower lid. Don't do this if you wear contact lenses.

6 To swell the bruise, stipple extra highlight on the areas shown. Don't blend it. Then, to add still more dimension to the makeup, run a little line of dark brown-red through the eyebrow to give a split brow.

BLACK SKIN

To create a black eye on black skin, follow the same routine, but use a black or very dark brown lining color (depending on the skin tone) instead of purple. Apply this first, then add the dark red-brown to it. If the skin is very dark, just use black liner, as the red won't show up. Highlight with a shade appropriate for black skins.

DISTORTED EYE

I Apply FOUNDATION and POWDER carefully. Cut a strip of Leuko-flex about 1½ to 2 inches long. Check the script to see which eye is damaged, then do a trial run, pulling the skin down to see how far the eyelid will stretch. Attach one end of the tape to the corner of the eyelid, stretch the tape, and press the other end onto the cheek.

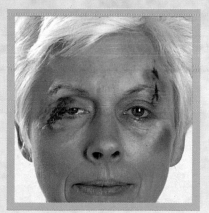

2 Color over the tape with brownish-red liner, stippling it on with your finger and adding darker areas where appropriate. Redden the tiredness shadow and HIGHLIGHT anywhere you feel should look puffy and swollen.

Makeup on Show

Some shows require a complete makeup design; a good example is *Cats*. Interestingly, the faces were created by the production designer, not by a makeup artist. After a few years, the females became less and less cat-like, and a makeup designer, Karen Dawson, was called in to create set faces for the various companies.

All the cats are individual, and the makeup is designed to indicate their character as well as to work with the costumes.

The first cat (1) is frisky and obviously female, with a clever combination of scarlet lips and a cat's muzzle. The second one (2) is a fierce tomcat with uptilted eyes and a determined chin. These makeups are done with facial water paints called Aquacolors which give a crisp definition on the face, can be mixed and faded, and are self-setting.

Starlight Express (3–5) is another example of stylized makeup. Here every member of the cast plays a train. The face designs are very angular, working against the facial structure and making them inhuman. Despite this, the female cars are cleverly feminine, and as in *Cats*, there is a sense of individuality working with the costume designs.

1

2

4

5

3

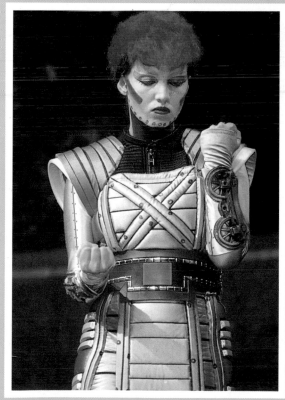

Makeup for Film and Television

Max Factor, Russian wig-maker and makeup master, created the first film makeup and won an Academy Award in 1926 for his achievement. Most of today's professional lines have their roots in Max Factor colors. Makeup for film and TV work has to be carefully blended, and shading and highlighting must be subtle. It has to combat the problems of people looking larger on camera and any redness of the skin being magnified, and, as with stage work, of the lighting draining color from the skin and making it look tired. Mandy Furlonger, well-known film and television makeup designer, contributed to this section.

Makeup for Women

Here we are aiming for a made-up look, with shading and highlighting to improve the face. All makeup designers have their own way of working, and the routine described here is different from that in the stage section. The guest makeup artist is Mandy Furlonger.

See also

Foundation p.12

Shading and highlighting p.15

Powder p.21

Rouge p.22

1 Fluid FOUNDATIONS work well for film and TV. Choose one that gives good cover and, if you need more, mix a little cream stick with the fluid. For medium to dark skins, choose a base close to the skin tone. Fair skins should use something deeper, or the face can look heavy. Take care to cover any pink areas, as they will be very noticeable on camera.

2 Cover any tiredness shadows under the eyes with a cream HIGHLIGHT, or a very pale cover stick. Pat it gently with a fingertip so that it doesn't stand out too strongly. Hide any small skin blemishes with highlight applied with a small brush. If the skin is in really bad condition, use a thicker cream stick or a camouflage cream to match the foundation.

3 Carefully SHADE the cheekbone hollows if they need more structure, but don't overdo it or it will show. Also use a little shader to improve the nose. Older women, and those with small eyes, will need shading on the browbones. POWDER well with a velour puff.

4 Brush the eyebrows and fill in the shape. Use a pencil or a powder eyebrow makeup in dark brown or charcoal if they are very thin or too short. Powder eye shadows look softer on camera. Because the model has big eyelids, a pale shadow is used from the eyebrows to the eyelashes. A socket shadow emphasizes the top of the eyelids. Without it the browbone looks too prominent.

5 Define under the eyes with the same color brown used for the sockets. Take a little eyeliner across the roots of the top lashes, widening it slightly toward the outer ends. You can also use a little under the eyes. To prevent powder shadow falling on other areas of the face, hold a powder puff close to the eye, or put a layer of powder under the eyes, brushing it off later.

6 Darken the outer edges of the eyelids with a deeper brown, using a soft brush, to give more depth. The shadows should blend into each other. Apply powder blusher on and under the cheekbones, using a natural color that gives a soft glow to the cheeks. If the jaw needs definition, take some blusher along the edge of the bone and under it, using a shading color.

7 Apply brown rather than black mascara to the eyelashes unless they are naturally very dark. Then brush or comb them through to separate the hairs and remove any lumps. Outline the lips and fill them in, making a natural shape. Avoid dull, flat colors or anything with a lot of blue in it, and make sure the lipstick tones with the blusher – the camera will magnify any difference.

African-American Women

This basic makeup for dark-skinned and black women balances the features, enhances the eyes, and gives an attractive made-up look for the camera. Once again, the principles are the same as for stage work, but the colors change and the result is more subtle.

See also

Foundation p.12

Shading and highlighting p.15

Powder p.21

Rouge p.22

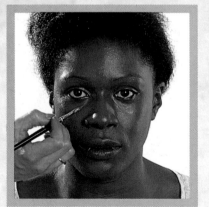

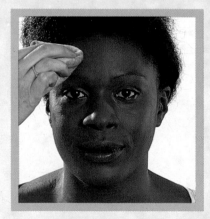

1 As for the stage makeup, choose a FOUNDATION that matches the coloring. For very dark skin use one with a reddish tone, which lifts the uniform depth of color. Here the makeup is a compact cream from a black fashion brand. HIGHLIGHT out the tiredness shadows with a yellowish-toned highlight. If the skin is really dark, make sure the highlight isn't too pale in contrast with the foundation.

2 The SHADING and HIGHLIGHTING to improve the facial structure is done later with powder products, so set the makeup now. Use translucent POWDER if you want a sheen to the skin – darker translucents are available. For a velvety look, choose a matte powder. Because the skin has a natural shine, powder very thoroughly.

3 If the eyebrows are too thin, the browbones stand out and take attention away from the eyes. Black cake eyeliner gives good definition. Use a good-quality long brush and check the amount on it before drawing the shape. Color and shape the eyes with powder eye shadow in neutral colors like this gold, or copper. Blend it all over the eyelid, and add a little rusty shimmer close to the nose.

4 Apply a charcoal socket shadow along the edge of the browbone to strengthen the top line of the eyelid, blending the edge to avoid a hard line. Add a little black or charcoal powder shadow to the outer corners of the eyelids and under the eyes. Soften the color with a clean brush or sponge tip, especially on the lids.

5 Add SHADING to give better shape to the cheekbones with a very dark brown powder shadow. Use a matte color; those with a built-in sheen will not work. If you need stronger shaping, use creams as shown in BASIC SHADING, powdering afterward.

6 Blusher helps to break up the even darkness of the face and highlight the cheeks. On really deep skin tones, you need one with rich pigments for it to show. Choose a color that tones with the lipstick.

7 As the mouth and lips are usually full, bright lipstick will look too strong. Use a rich, deep color like this one. Draw in the outline with pencil and then fill in the color.

Oriental Women

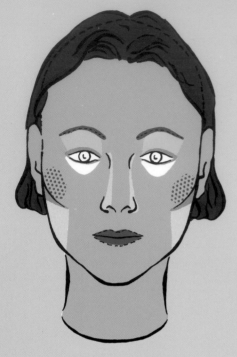

Oriental faces, with their deep-set eyes, need careful, subtle makeup to show the natural beauty. This is a classic natural look, using a small amount of rouge and lip color.

See also ☞

Foundation p.12

Shading and highlighting p.15

Eye shapes p.29

Powder p.21

False eyelashes p.26

Rouge p.22

1 Choose a FOUNDATION to tone with the skin color; a yellowish tone needs a warmer base color, but beware of using one that is too pink. A fine cream makeup or a fluid is suitable. Oriental eyes often have noticeable under-lids with natural shadows beneath them. To reduce them and balance this area, use an ivory-toned highlighter and blend it on the shadow area.

2 Because the face is broad and flat, the SHADING needs to be very specific. Powder shaders are too imprecise; you need a cream liner to shape the face. Use a soft, dark brown shadow under the cheekbones and down the sides of the nose to strengthen the bridge. Use a softer amount of brown blended over the sides of the jaw under the cheek shading or the face will look very square.

3 If the eyes are very narrow, shade the browbone as well, and add a soft socket shadow [SEE EYE SHAPES]. Use a pale translucent POWDER, making sure that you set the eyelids especially well in preparation for fake lashes later. Blend a pale, warm brown shadow from the brows to the edges of the eyelids.

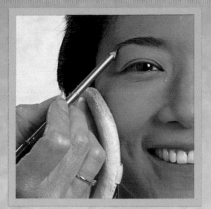

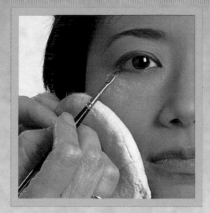

4 Define the eyebrows with a pencil, powder brow makeup or cake liner. Black might seem to be the appropriate color, but sometimes charcoal looks softer and better. Make sure the eyebrows are long enough or the browbone area will look puffy.

5 Edge the top and bottom lids with dark brown eyeliner. Black looks hard on camera and narrows the eyes. Powder liners like this can cause shadows under the eyes, so put a layer of face powder under them and brush it off when the lines are in place.

6 Mascara the top and bottom lashes. If they aren't very thick, use dark brown to give a lusher look. A pair of natural-looking FALSE EYELASHES will help to emphasize the eyes. If you can see the glue when you have applied them, re-do the top eye line with cake liner.

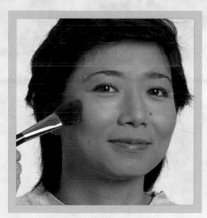

7 Brush a soft, peach-toned blusher over the cheek shading and the cheekbones, being careful not to take it onto the natural fullness close to the nose, which will give heaviness, or up into the temples, which will make the face look wide. Apply a warm-toned lipstick with a little red in it. Oriental lips are quite full, and a pale color would make them look too big compared with the eyes.

Hispanic and Indian Women

The deeper-toned Hispanic face needs little enhancement for the camera. This low-key makeup balances the features and emphasizes the eyes. The richness of the Indian skin tone also needs little makeup, and this subtle routine lifts the tiredness shadows and shows the beauty of the eyes.

See also

Foundation p.12

Shading and highlighting p.15

Powder p.21

Rouge p.22

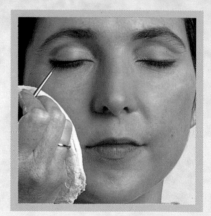

1 The model has an olive-toned skin with some high color on the cheekbones. A dense-textured fluid FOUNDATION with a yellowish tone gives good cover and matches the natural coloring. Blend it with a slightly damp sponge and use a wide, flat brush for awkward areas. HIGHLIGHT the tiredness shadows with an ivory fluid or cream stick. A fluid will need to be quite thick in texture to hide really dark shadows.

2 POWDER with translucent loose powder, then color the eyebrows, improving the shape as you work. Since many Hispanic women have naturally thick, dark brows, be careful not to overdraw them. Here a black pencil defines the arch and strengthens the ends of the eyebrows. Really thick brows just need brushing through with a little spray gel to hold their shape.

3 Leave the eyelid without eye-shadow, but use a dark brown powder shader to emphasize the socket, looking directly ahead to get the correct position. Fade the same brown onto the outer corners of the top lids and take a fine line of it along the roots of the lower lashes. Take a thin line of black cake or liquid eyeliner along the roots of the top eyelashes, fading at the outer corners.

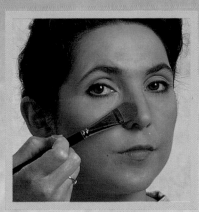

4 Mascara the eyelashes, using black, and brush through them well afterward. This face needs minimal SHADING. A medium brown powder shader gives more shape under the cheekbones, softens the sides of the jaw line, and slims the nose. Make sure there is no stickiness on the skin before you apply it, or the shader will catch on it and become patchy.

5 Blend a rusty-toned blusher over the cheekbones and slightly over the cheek shading. Powder to soften hard edges. A lip-line pencil helps to give a clear outline for the lipstick. Choose a color that matches the stick. With a poorly defined lower lip, paint a little foundation around the shape and powder it before using the pencil. Fill in with soft red lipstick.

6 Our Indian model has a compact cream FOUNDATION to even the skin tone. Use a dark brown powder SHADER under the cheekbones on darker skin, down the sides of the nose, and across its tip. Enhance the eyes with a pearlized gray-brown eye shadow and fade a charcoal socket shadow onto the outer eyelid and under the eyes. Finish with a deep, rusty shade of blusher and a warm-toned lipstick.

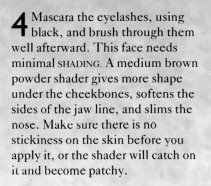

Makeup for Men

On film and television, all men need minimal makeup – just enough to cover any problems, even out the skin tone, and define any features that need strengthening. The makeup should be unnoticeable.

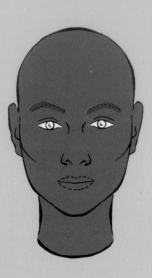

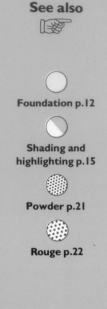

See also

Foundation p.12

Shading and highlighting p.15

Powder p.21

Rouge p.22

1 Choose a FOUNDATION which matches the skin tone but has a little warmth – red – in it, as it will film better. You can use a cream foundation, a little cake makeup, or a fluid. See also the section on basic SHADING and HIGHLIGHTING if the face needs more shape.

2 Shine is an actor's worst enemy on camera. The skin has a natural shine, so if you don't powder well, the makeup will become greasy under the warm lights, and the face will look shapeless. This is a medium brown, translucent loose POWDER. Powder the whole face carefully with a puff or cotton ball.

3 The model's eyebrows need more definition from the center to the outer ends. To strengthen the color of the brows, darken them with a black pencil or cake-liner, drawing in little hairs among the real ones for a natural effect.

1 Apply a FOUNDATION close to the actor's natural coloring. We have used a fluid, but a thin layer of cake makeup is a quick way to do it. Use just enough to smooth the skin, remembering to blend it over the ears and down the neck a little. If more body shows, use cake makeup on it.

2 A little shadow under the eyes can make the face more masculine, but if the actor looks really tired or needs to appear younger, you will need HIGHLIGHTS. Apply it in the same place as for stage makeup. Set the makeup carefully with loose translucent powder – it wastes valuable shooting time if you are constantly retouching to control the shine.

3 If the lower lid needs definition, take a line of brown cake eyeliner or pencil along under the lower lashes [SEE PAGE 47]. Men with dark eyelashes probably won't need it. If you use a line, fade it carefully. If you need a little more color, add powder blusher in the natural position described in the ROUGE section. For caucasian skins, the color should be more subtle than that used for the stage.

Characterization – Victorian Trollop

On film and television, obvious makeup is often used to express character, as in this interpretation of a Victorian prostitute. Nineteenth-century ladies worked hard to look fair-skinned, but the urban poor were naturally pale from their unhealthy lives.

See also

Foundation p.12

Shading and highlighting p.15

Powder p.21

Rouge p.22

Special effects p.88

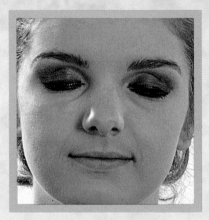

1 Use a very pale FOUNDATION, like this ivory, to give the skin pallor, ending it at the jaw line. Add SHADING to create tiredness shadows and lines from the nose to the mouth, painting on a little HIGHLIGHT to make them work with the lighting. Faces seemed rounder in this period, so unless you are plump, don't shade and highlight for structure. POWDER heavily with a pale, matte, loose powder.

2 Draw black eyebrows in a thin line or heavily darken the natural shape. Greasepaint, artists' pencils, or even black boot polish were used in Victorian times. Here we have used black cake eyeliner.

3 Heavy, bright blue eye shadow gives a cheap period look to the eyes, taken right over the lids and close up to the eyebrows. Cream shadow gives a more authentic look than powder – the Victorians used greasepaint. Powder if you use cream shadow. Draw a heavy black line right around the eyes with a pencil or, for a smudged look, a grease liner. Mascara is optional, as Victorians didn't have any.

4 Prostitutes ROUGED their faces heavily with theatrical makeup. Use bright pink or red blusher, or try a little lipstick rubbed on the center of the cheeks in a round, doll-like shape. Actresses of this period used something called Spanish wool, while Society ladies had "secret rouges."

5 Lips were rouged with grease-paint in very basic colors, so use the brightest red you can find and draw a rounded, bow-shaped lip line, smudging it for extra effect. You can, of course, use lipstick.

6 Always check to see how the makeup is progressing by stepping back from it. A little white eye shadow under the eyebrows makes the eyes look even more made up. It is optional, but it adds to the theatricality of the makeup.

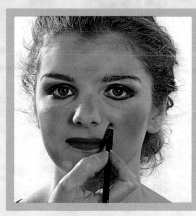

7 Dirty the face, neck, and hands with grease or cake eyeliner. Add a beauty spot in a desperate attempt at elegance and make the hair messy, perhaps half-held with cheap ribbons. To complete the effect, add a BRUISE, as here, or small CUTS and a BLACK EYE. Use nicotine tooth enamel to dirty the teeth, but not if they are capped.

Dickensian Gent

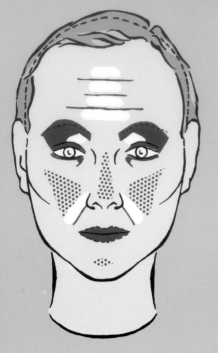

In TV and film work, actors are cast to type according to their appearance, and the character is then built up bit by bit. Here is an example of a Victorian gentleman, featuring the application of side whiskers. The aim is for a plump, jolly character, whose enjoyment of a glass or two of good port is reflected in his face.

See also

Foundation p.13

Shading and highlighting p.15

Powder p.21

Aging p.62

False hair p.24

1 This character is a jolly Victorian gentleman, and as our model has naturally warm coloring, no base was used. Fair or sallow skins will need a reddish-toned FOUNDATION to achieve this coloring, but pale men should adjust the foundation to suit their own skin tones. Add SHADING and HIGHLIGHTING as needed, adding extra to fatten the NOSE if necessary.

2 The model has interesting natural eyebrows which work well for this character, but need a little more definition. If you don't use foundation and are using a pencil for this, POWDER the area first, or it may slide on the shiny skin and look too heavy. With heavy brows, brush a little spirit gum through them to lift the shape.

3 Define under the eyelid with a faded brown line, and strengthen natural age lines with dark brown pencil. If there are no natural lines, add some for AGING, remembering to keep the effect subtle. Highlight to strengthen the lines, using the same color as for theater. Highlights must be wider than lines to avoid the suggestion of stripes on the face. Blend carefully.

4 Powder with translucent POWDER, taking particular care just in front of the ears and down to the jaw line where the whiskers will be. Stipple brownish-red cream liner over the cheeks and the end of the nose for broken veins. We've used a stipple sponge rather than a finger. Take care not to finish up with squares of redness on the cheeks.

5 Glue on the side whiskers [SEE PAGE 25], pinning up any long hair before you start, so the whiskers appear to come right up into the natural hair. Paint spirit gum where they are to go and press the false pieces into position using a small dry sponge. Make sure the lace base is completely stuck to the skin.

6 Hold the whiskers in place as they dry and then comb the real hair over the top. If it is very short or thinning, brush on a little cake eyeliner to fill in any gaps. If the side whiskers are a little different from the natural hair color, mascara them to match. A little highlight can be used on non-matching tones of gray.

7 Adjust the hair according to the period – here it has been darkened at the sides with cake eyeliner and combed forward. A theatrical spray tint can be used for darkening – hold the can at arm's length as you spray, and protect the skin with a tissue.

Aging Using Old Age Stipple

It is difficult to age a face on camera using highlight and shading unless it already has a certain amount of looseness. Foam rubber pieces and latex are used instead, and the simplest way is with Old Age Stipple. The model is being aged to create the character of Miss Havisham from Dickens' Great Expectations, *an old lady left at the altar in her youth who still wears her wedding dress. To retain the illusion of youth, she paints her face.*

See also

Foundation p.12

Shading and highlighting p.15

Powder p.21

Rouge p.22

Wigs p.27

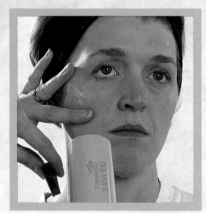

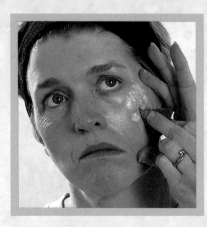

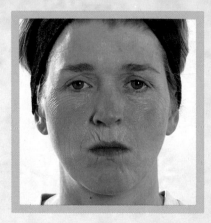

1 Lay out everything you need before you begin – a bottle of Old Age Stipple (liquid latex), a rubber sponge, a brush or two, and a hair dryer with a small nozzle. Pour some latex into a saucer ready to use, and tone the face. You must stretch the skin you want to wrinkle before you apply it, so do that with one hand and sponge on the latex with the other. Holding the skin, dry it with a hair dryer set on cool.

2 The eye areas are particularly important as the skin there loosens early in our lives. Stretch the delicate skin gently, lifting the eyebrows to work on the browbone, being careful not to drip latex into the eyes. You can build up two or three layers of latex, but make sure they don't have thick edges. In tight areas, paint it on with a brush.

3 To help stretch the mouth, pad inside the top and bottom lips with large pieces of sponge, stipple on the latex and dry thoroughly. When you take the sponge out, the mouth will look lined.

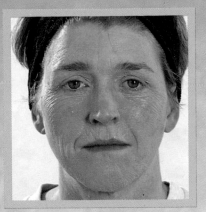

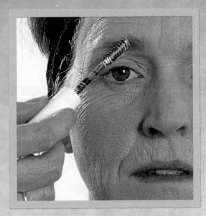

4 Stretch the cheeks firmly toward the ears, stipple over the smile lines, dry, and add another coat. Release the skin and see the effect. On the forehead, pull the skin up, stretching it outward between the eyebrows. Every stretch will produce fine lines and wrinkles, but not unless you keep the skin stretched as the latex dries. This is how it looks after three layers.

5 When you feel you have the right degree of age, you can begin coloring the face. Apply a paler than usual FOUNDATION lightly over the skin, add a little SHADING to strengthen the major lines, then POWDER. Whiten the eyebrows lightly to give a few gray hairs.

6 A little blue eye shadow on the eyelids is optional. If the eye folds need strengthening, brush on matte powder highlight. Apply a pink blusher low on the cheekbones to suggest a rouged face. Mascara the eyelashes with brownish-black and brush through them. It should look unnoticeable, as it didn't exist in this period. For an older look, omit the blue shadow and brush a little highlight onto the lashes.

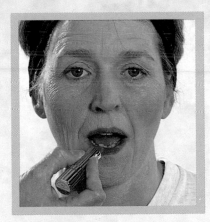

7 Dark red lipstick drawn in a thin shape makes the mouth look rouged but older; fuller lips would look too young. If you don't want the mouth to look made up, line the edges with a reddish-brown pencil and fade the color onto the lips. Finish with an untidy WIG.

Prosthetics

Prosthetics can be used to create stunning effects and are not particularly difficult, provided you follow the important rules given here and make sure that you read through all the steps carefully before you begin. Here we are casting a face in two stages, making a false nose and then using the prosthesis and false hair to create an evil gnome-like character makeup.

See also 👉

Restoration p.80

Foundation p.13

Powder p.21

False hair p.24

Wigs p.27

IMPORTANT Read through all the instructions carefully first.

Always work in a well-lit and well-ventilated room.

Lay out a table with everything you will need and cut the plaster bandage into 2½-inch strips.

Cover the floor and anything else nearby; this is a messy business.

Work with an assistant – this job needs two pairs of hands.

Check that the actor understands what is going to happen. He or she may feel claustrophobic.

Make sure there will be no interruptions.

FOR THE MODEL

A comfortable chair.

Protective clothing for the model, the assistant, and yourself.

Something to cover the hair, for example a swimming cap or shower cap.

EQUIPMENT/MATERIALS

Three large bowls (one shallow).

Several pitchers of water.

Alginate.

Plaster of Paris.

Several rolls of plaster bandage.

A piece of sacking or coarse fabric.

Petroleum jelly.

Towels.

A wooden spoon.

Wire or a piece of metal coat hanger.

Modeling wax or clay.

Two short pieces of plastic drinking straw.

A small, sharp modeling knife.

Paint brush.

Patience!

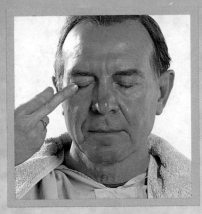

CASTING THE NEGATIVE

1 Cover the model's clothes, and tuck a towel around the neck. Apply a thin film of petroleum jelly over the face to stop the alginate from sticking to the skin, paying particular attention to the eyebrows and eyelashes (the model should close his or her eyes). Although we haven't here, cover the hair if it could fall in the face.

2 Quickly mix the alginate with water, as instructed on the pack, until it is thick but runny. Working quickly, cover the face with alginate starting at the forehead and working down one side, while your assistant does the other side. The alginate will run downward as you work. Fill in all the crevices of the nose, but leave the nostrils clear.

3 The assistant is stretching the nostrils to keep them clear before the top lip is covered. The alginate is runny enough to drip off the chin – if you are quick, you can scoop up the drips and use them. If it starts to set and you haven't covered the face thickly, peel off the alginate, check the petroleum jelly, and start again.

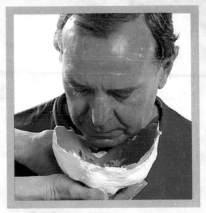

4 If you are inexperienced, put a drinking straw in each nostril before applying the plaster bandage. Make sure a bowl of water and the strips of plaster bandage are close at hand. Take a piece of bandage, dip it in the water, and smooth it on the face. You can work in any pattern as long as you cover all the alginate. We covered the hair now because the plaster was getting onto it.

5 Now the whole face has two or three layers of plaster bandage over it to support the alginate negative. Pay particular attention to the nose area – if it is unsupported, the alginate will split. The edges also need enough bandage on them to keep them firm.

6 Make sure the model is comfortable and the head supported while the plaster dries. It may take up to half an hour and feels warm as it dries. Keep checking on the model. When the plaster has set, it will feel cool. Check the cast edges are loose and ask the model to wiggle the face while you carefully lift off the cast, supporting it with your other hand.

Casting the Positive

Grease any plaster bandage sticking up above the alginate with a little petroleum jelly to prevent the new plaster from sticking to it. Put a small towel into a large, shallow bowl to support the negative mold while you fill it with plaster, or support the mask on a ring of clay. Fill the nostril holes with wax or clay, raised above the level of plaster inside the mask.

7 Protect your hands with barrier cream to prevent the plaster from becoming ingrained. Fill a bowl with water and pour plaster into the center until it rises above the surface. Keep pouring until all the water is absorbed. Leave it for a minute, then hand mix it, breaking up any lumps. When it is thick but runny, bang the bowl on the floor to raise any air bubbles, then begin filling the mask with plaster.

8 We are holding up the mask so you can see inside it, but you will have it supported on a table. Don't pour plaster into the mask to begin with as this will cause air bubbles which will pit the surface. Instead, flick it in, covering the whole surface thinly.

9 Then scoop up more plaster with your hand and pour it into the mask until it is about 1 inch thick all over. Use a brush to spread it evenly. It will start to set immediately, and as it does, score it with the knife to give a key for the next step.

10 Quickly wipe your hands, pull pieces of thread from the sacking and lay them on the plaster. This will strengthen the finished cast and provide another key for the next layer. Take care that no threads stick out of the mold, and work quickly before the plaster sets completely.

11 Build up another layer of sacking and plaster as before, again working quickly before the plaster sets.

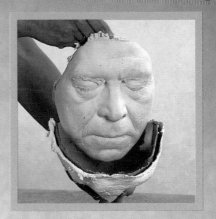

12 Mix up a new batch of thicker plaster and pour it over the sacking, spreading it with your hands until you have a total depth of 2 inches of plaster all over. Don't fill it right to the top because its weight would distort the alginate.

13 Make a little hook with the wire or coat hanger and place it at the top of the face to make it easier to lift the positive out of the mold when it has dried.

14 When the cast is dry, carefully loosen the edge with a knife, but don't dig into the plaster. Gently ease it out of the mold, holding it by the hook. Fill any air bubbles holes on the surface carefully with a little thin plaster, and scrape off any lumps with your knife or modeling tool.

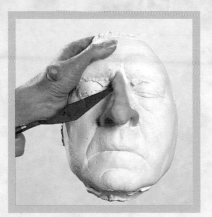

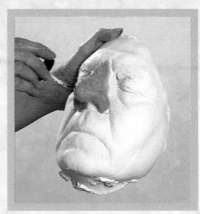

MODELING NEW FEATURES

15 We are going to use the cast of this face to model a nose. Whatever you are going to make, first find a photograph of what you want, then model the new feature onto the positive, using mortician's wax or clay. Shape the nose with modeling tools and make certain the edges are absolutely smooth.

16 Lightly grease the new nose with petroleum jelly. To build a strong nose, paint twenty layers of cap plastic or latex onto the cast – if it is too thin, it will tear easily. To strengthen it, tear single sheets of facial tissues into pieces and lay them between the layers of latex, letting each layer dry before adding another tissue. Keep the latex edges very fine.

17 To remove the prosthesis from the cast, powder around the edges and ease it off with a fine palette knife, then powder it well inside and out. Tone the skin well. Apply spirit gum and fit the nose to the face, pressing down the edges well.

The Gnome

This makeup uses familiar materials, but applied over the false nose.

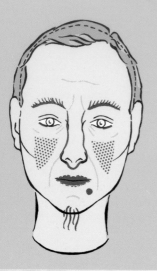

18 Professionals use acetone to dissolve edges into the skin, but don't do this if the skin is dry or sensitive. To color the nose, you can either use a tinted powder which matches the foundation between the layers, or color the latex itself by scraping the correct color cake makeup into it.

19 Brush spirit gum through the eyebrows and comb them up, flattening them against the skin ready for the fake brows later in the makeup. If you are sensitive to spirit gum, use a medical adhesive instead. Hold a brush handle across the eyebrows to keep the hairs flat as they dry.

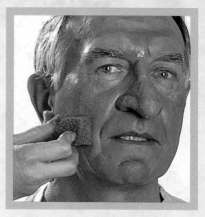

20 Now color the face and nose with a dark FOUNDATION. You may need to mix colors to do this on the nose, and you must use creams, as fluids and cakes are difficult to blend on latex.

21 Deepen and lengthen the smile lines, frown lines, and the curve of the chin below the lips with dark brown to make the face look sour and a little sinister. Blend the lines to make them look real.

22 Stipple a darker base over the cheeks with a sponge to weather the face, and add some brownish-red EF9 for ruddiness. POWDER only lightly, as a little shine will highlight the natural folds of the face.

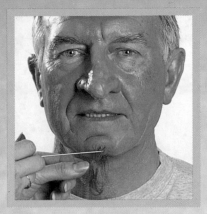

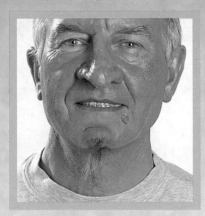

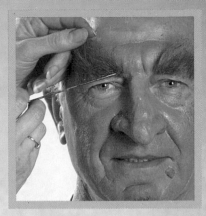

23 To make a whiskery chin, press out a few strands of crêpe hair and glue long straggly pieces onto it. Press the ends firmly to the chin with the handle of a comb or a brush to secure them [SEE BEARDS].

24 Make a wart with a small ball of mortician's wax and glue it onto an appropriate position with eyelash adhesive, or use a latex wart or even a Rice Krispie. Color the wart with a little light or dark brown liner and powder it.

25 False eyebrows add to the general hairiness. These are made of crêpe wool on a strip of toupee tape and pressed over the real brows. The tape is adhesive on both sides, but make sure the eyebrow area is not greasy or the tape will not stick. Hide shiny areas with dark brown powder shadow.

26 Now put on the WIG. This one has a hair-lace front going across the forehead and down to the ears, and is held in place by dabs of matte spirit gum. Finally, discolor the teeth with nicotine-colored tooth enamel. Dry the teeth and paint on the enamel, keeping the mouth open until it dries. Again, don't use tooth enamel on capped teeth.

Special Effects

See also

Complicated-looking effects, like this gory road accident victim and horrific burn, can be simple to create. This burn is on an arm, but it could be anywhere on the body. Read through both makeups before starting, and use reference photographs if possible. The actor should be in costume first to avoid smudging the makeup.

Advice on using fake blood follows on page 123.

Foundation p.13

Blood p.123

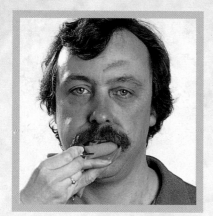

1 If you are using FOUNDATION, choose a pale color to give the effect of shock. Paint a little blue liner into the tiredness shadows and smile lines, and a line of faded blue across the forehead. Highlight the lines and each side of the blue on the forehead with petroleum jelly. Tuck a piece of sponge into the mouth down past the lower teeth; too big a piece will look odd and hinder speech. Position it carefully.

2 Add areas of red liner to give BRUISING and small CUTS to the face. Think what a real accident victim looks like and try to recreate it as realistically as possible. Here, for realism, the impact has more effect on one side than the other.

3 Paint spirit gum over the end of one eyebrow and let it dry. It clogs the hair and, when colored, looks like congealed blood coming from a split eyebrow. When the gum has dried, color it with black grease liner, then dab areas of black onto the nose. Paint red wound filler (or dark red liner) over it and the glued eyebrow. To suggest swelling, brush a powder shine onto the nose and around the mouth.

 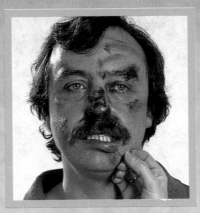 

4 If the actor has a mustache or beard, thickly paint spirit gum on part of it and let it dry. Color it with black grease liner and add "blood." Paint red liner along the top lid close to the eyelashes, under the eyes and in the tiredness area at the outer corners. Fade it to soften the color.

5 Now distort the mouth. Paint rigid collodion under the lower lip on the same side as the sponge, and press the lip down onto the collodion to stick it to the skin. For extra hold, cut a strip of Leukoflex, wipe off any moisture on the lip and press one end of the tape onto it and the other end onto the chin. This will hold the mouth firmly in place.

6 Color the distorted lip with black grease, then add more to the skin under the mouth. Only grease makeup will adhere to the moist lip. Dry the lower teeth with a tissue and paint red tooth enamel over the roots (it won't work on wet teeth). For the sake of hygiene, avoid using the little brush in the bottle. Gel the hair with your hands for a matted effect.

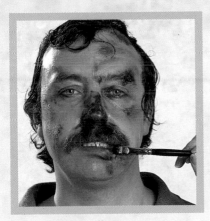

7 Finally, add a little more black in the corner of the mouth and dribble some "blood" from a cut so that it runs down the neck. Leave this to the last possible moment to keep it fresh-looking. Dab black grease and wound filler into the hair where the wound is supposed to be.

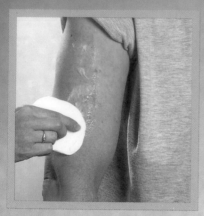

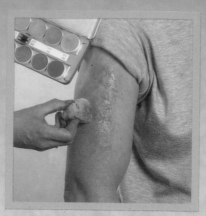

1 To match the face, apply a thin wash of cake makeup to the arm, then paint spirit gum over a large area. Drag a piece of absorbent cotton across the wet gum, allowing trails to stick, to give the typical stringy look of a serious burn. Always use 100% cotton, as the fiber type has silky strands which cause problems. When the first layer of gum is dry, add another layer and allow it to dry.

2 Apply D32 camouflage cream over the whole area with a damp sponge. The dull pink color gives the look of raw tissue, and is also useful for covering bruises and beard shadows.

3 Add a brighter red to several areas of the burn to give depth. Sponge over the red areas to blend the colors together a little. Use a natural sponge, as the open holes help to give texture to the burn.

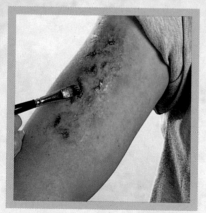

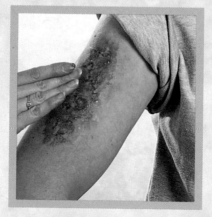

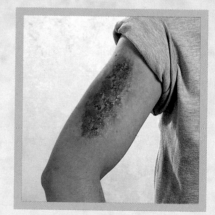

4 Now add a little black grease liner to give a charred effect on the wound – too much will spoil the effect. You could also use a black powder shadow. Sponge the black a little and pick off any over-colored cotton fluff.

5 Finally, to make the burn look as if it is oozing, pat glycerin over the whole area with your hand. As a general rule for makeup, do not use too much, as you can always build it up later.

6 This is the finished effect. Stand back from the makeup to check its progress, and add layers and color until you have the desired effect.

Blood

Nowadays you can buy different types of "blood" over the counter. Here are a few types available, plus a recipe for creating your own.

PLASTIC BLOOD (TUPLAST)

This comes in a small tube in either a dark blood color or transparent, and is used mainly for cuts. Ideal for quick work, squeeze it straight onto the skin and shape it before it sets. It is used extensively in TV work.

POWDER BLOOD

This comes in tubs and is useful when you need lots of blood. It is mixed with water, or can be thrown around and then sprayed with water.

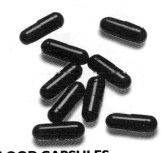

EYE BLOOD

This is squeezed into the eye like drops and gives a highly dramatic, though short-lived, effect, immediately turning the white of the eye scarlet. It only lasts a few minutes, however, before being diluted by the natural fluid of the eye. It must not be used with contact lenses.

JELLY BLOOD (WOUND FILLER)

This comes in various colors and is used to give a wet blood effect. It is good for filling large wounds and for matting in hair.

BLOOD CAPSULES

Used in the mouth, these require sharp teeth to bite through the gelatin and release the blood, which then combines with saliva and foams. They won't work if the mouth is dry.

LIQUID BLOOD

This is the most widely used type. All companies make it, and it comes in various colors suitable for film, TV, and theater. Most makes are washable. Don't apply it too far ahead because it gradually dries and eventually begins to flake.

SCURF BLOOD

This is made from liquid latex, and is good in makeups where the effect is to be picked at.

TOOTH BLOOD

This is a red tooth enamel which is painted onto the teeth after they have been dried with a tissue, to give the appearance of bleeding gums. It stays on until rubbed off with damp absorbent cotton.

DO-IT-YOURSELF BLOOD

You will need: Baby oil, red grease lining color, brown and blue lining colors. Put a small spoonful of red lining color into a flameproof bowl and place the bowl over a pan of gently boiling water until the color melts. Gradually add the baby oil, stirring it into the liner until you have a blood-like consistency. If you need to adjust the color, add a little brown or blue liner. The EF9 liner used in this book makes an excellent dark blood color.
Note: Being oil-based, this "blood" doesn't set, and smudges easily.

Makeup on Show

Prosthetic makeup is probably the most complicated of all makeup techniques, requiring considerable expertise to create really good effects. These photographs show some of the steps in the process. To create this she-wolf, a cast is taken of the actress's own features, and the muzzle built from that and recast. (pages 114–19.)

Here is the actress as she really is (1). In the second photograph (2) her hair is covered with a bald cap and the makeup artist is making final adjustments to the prosthesis muzzle. The muzzle and mouth are carefully fitted and glued to the face with rubber adhesive. After this the edges are dissolved into the skin with acetone. In the final photograph (3), the whole face has been made up with bald cap grease and powdered. The muzzle end is darkened a little and the eyes outlined. Wisps of hair are laid on the head and sides of the face.

The more elaborate wolf (4) has an extended muzzle and teeth. Hair is laid over the prostheses. The pig (5), created by Mandy Furlonger for a TV version of Beatrix Potter's *Little Pig Robinson*, has glycerin on the snout and around the eyes to give a snuffling look.

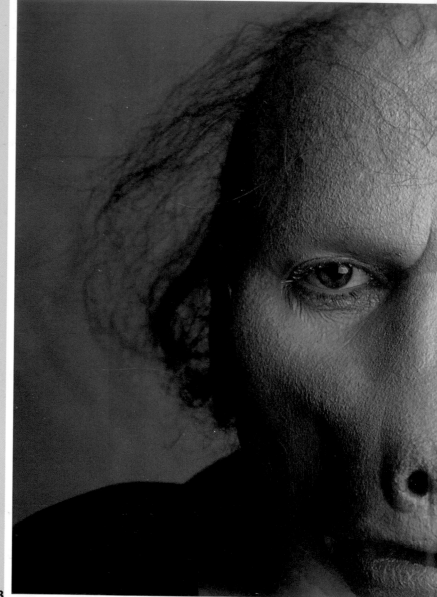

3

Index

Credits

In gratitude to two brilliant makeup artists, Eve Gardiner and Douglas Young of Max Factor, who taught me the basics of my craft and gave so generously of their expertise. Thank you.

Makeup Charles H. Fox Ltd; **Wigs** Derek Easton; **Wardrobe/jewelry** Cassie, Giulia Hetherington, Marie Hood, The London Academy of Music and Dramatic Art, Muriel Peattie, Dolly Swinfield, Ray Swinfield; **Secretarial support** Marian Titchmarsh

Quarto and the author would like to thank the following people who kindly agreed to be models:
Robin Coleridge pages 110–11; **Sarah Cosgrove** pages 42–3, 104–5; **Rosemary Denny** pages 58–9, 88–9, 92–3; **David Edwards** pages 25–6, 27; **Jim Forrester** page 52; **Laura Forrester** pages 23, 54–7, 86–7; **David Furlonger** pages 120–2; **Clare Green** pages 50–1, 53; **Jodie Kent** pages 83, 98–9, 108–9; **Miles Lanham** pages 1, 30, 80–2, 84–5; **Ola Osimbi** pages 24–5, 45, 106; **Catherine Raynor-Brown** pages 18–19, 64–9, 90, 91; **Sadie Rule** pages 6, 12, 13, 15, 19, 20, 22–3, 28, 32–7, 72–3, 76–9; **Frank Taylor** pages 60–3, 90, 96, 107, 115–19; **Pam Taylor** pages 112–13; **Minu Verma** pages 21, 43, 105; **Nick Wall** pages 13, 16–17, 44, 46–9, 70–1, 74–5; **Beverley Williamson** pages 38–9, 100–1; **Zarni Win** pages 40–1, 102–3

Photographic Credits
Every effort has been made to clear copyright of photographs. Quarto would like to apologize if any omissions have been made.
Sipa/Rex Features page 54 (bottom left); Stills/Rex Features page 94 (1 & 2); Tim Rooke/Rex Features page 95 (3); Clive Dixon/Rex Features page 95 (4); Phil Loftus/Capital Pictures page 95 (5); Stephen Lovell-Davis pages 124–5 (1, 2, 3, 4); Gerald Sunderland page 125 (5)

Selected Suppliers
London Charles H. Fox Ltd, 22 Tavistock Street, Covent Garden WC2E 7PY; Theatre Zoo, 21 Earlham Street, Cambridge Circus WC2H 9LL; Screen Face, 24 Powis Terrace, W11 1JJ; **USA** Kryolan Corporation, 132 Ninth Street, San Francisco, California, CA 94103; **Australia** Johanne Santry, 7 Batemans Road, Gladesville, NSW 2111; **Germany** Kryolan, Papierstraße 10, D-1000, Berlin S1